Appreciating Poetry

PRENTICE HALL
Upper Saddle River, New Jersey
Needham, Massachusetts

PRENTICE HALL

Acknowledgments

Grateful acknowledgment is made to the following for copyrighted material:

Absey & Co.
"Just People" by Kathi Appelt from *Just People and Other Poems for Young Readers.* Copyright 1997, Absey & Co. Reprinted by permission of Absey & Co.

Samuel Allen
"To Satch" by Samuel Allen. © Samuel Allen. Reprinted by permission of Samuel W. Allen.

Coleman Barks
"The Lame Goat" from *The Essential Rumi* by Jalal al-Din Rumi, translated by Coleman Barks with John Moyne, A. J. Arberry, and Reynold Nicholson. Copyright © 1995 by Coleman Barks. Reprinted by permission of Coleman Barks.

Catherine Beston Barnes
"On a Night of Snow" from *Night and the Cat* by Elizabeth Coatsworth, copyright 1950 The Macmillan Company. Reprinted by permission of Catherine Beston Barnes.

Elizabeth Barnett, literary executor for Edna St. Vincent Millay
"Come along in then, little girl!" from *From a Very Little Sphinx* from COLLECTED POEMS OF EDNA ST. VINCENT MILLAY, HarperCollins. Copyright © 1929, 1956 by Edna St. Vincent Millay and Norma Millay Ellis. All rights reserved. Reprinted by permission of Elizabeth Barnett, literary executor.

D.C. Berry
"On Reading Poems To A Senior Class At South High" by D.C. Berry. Copyright © D.C.B. Reprinted by permission of the author.

(Acknowledgments continue on p. 153.)

Contents

Contents

Contents

Contents

Ponder This   "I am puzzled"

Introduction

Introductions to poetry books so often begin with an attempt to answer the question, "Why do people read poetry?" Why should this book be any different? Why do people read poetry? In other words, why bother to read writing that may be harder to understand than simple, straightforward prose, and that is written in a form so different from the way we ordinarily speak? People have been reading and enjoying poetry for thousands of years, so there must be a reason. Perhaps the best way to answer the question, "Why do people read poetry?" is by asking another question: Have you ever noticed that when you have strong feelings you sometimes have trouble expressing them? That you just can't put them into words? One reason for reading poetry is that it seems able to express feelings in a more vivid and precise way than ordinary language. For example, here's a line of simple, straightforward prose that's easy to understand and makes perfect sense:

> I am happy.

Reading those words might give you a nice feeling, but they don't really express what it feels like to be happy. In contrast, read these lines from a poem in this book, "A Blessing." The poet, James Wright, tells you:

> ... if I stepped out of my body I would break
> Into blossom.

Those lines give you a much better idea of what happiness feels like. In addition, they give you a picture to keep in your head and remember when you're feeling happy yourself.

Here's another question. Have you ever noticed that words for feelings are hard to define? For example, completing the sentence, "Happiness is _____" is a pretty tough assignment. But a poem by Stephen Dunn called "Happiness," which you'll also find in this book, says that happiness is a place with

> the roads leading to a castle
> that doesn't exist.
> But there it is, as promised

Not bad, right? So another part of our answer is that poetry can define important concepts and feelings that ordinary language can't seem to quite grasp.

Here's one more reason for reading poetry. It uses language, sometimes in surprising or unexpected ways, to make you see things in a more vivid way than ordinary speech. Consider these examples from this book:

Langston Hughes's way of saying, "Life isn't easy":

Life for me ain't been no crystal stair

Evelyn Tooley Hunt's way of expressing the comforting presence of a mother:

When she comes sweet-talking in the room,
she warms us

Eve Merriam's way of saying she's in love:

...I am putting a hat on my head
so the flaming meteors
in my hair
will hardly show.

Karl Shapiro's description of a dead bug:

It was a mite that held itself most dear,
So small I could have drowned it with a tear.

And finally, William Shakespeare's way of describing trees in winter:

Bare ruined choirs where late the sweet birds sang.

For more examples, turn the pages of this book and see what captures your imagination. Find lines that say exactly what you were thinking, but couldn't quite put into words. Find out why the Tunisian poet Muhammad al-Ghuzzi writes that, for a poet,

...the whole world is a sky-blue butterfly
And words are the nets to capture it.

Love of Life
"Swift things are beautiful"

Happiness

Stephen Dunn

A state you must dare not enter
   with hopes of staying,
quicksand in the marshes, and all

the roads leading to a castle
   that doesn't exist.
But there it is, as promised.

with its perfect bridge above
   the crocodiles,
and its doors forever open.

Listen to the Mustn'ts

Shel Silverstein

Listen to the MUSTN'TS, child,
Listen to the DON'TS
Listen to the SHOULDN'TS
The IMPOSSIBLES, the WON'TS
Listen to the NEVER HAVES
Then listen close to me—
Anything can happen, child,
ANYTHING can be.

the poet

lucille clifton

i beg my bones to be good but
    they keep clicking music and
i spin in the center of myself
    a foolish frightful woman
moving my skin against the wind and
    tap dancing for my life.

A Boy's Head

Miroslav Holub

Translated by Ian Milner

In it there is a space-ship
and a project
for doing away with piano lessons.

And there is
Noah's ark,
which shall be first.

And there is
an entirely new bird,
an entirely new hare,
an entirely new bumble-bee.

There is a river
that flows upwards.

There is a multiplication table

There is anti-matter

And it just cannot be trimmed

I believe
that only what cannot be trimmed
is a head.

There is much promise
in the circumstance
that so many people have heads.

Song

Eskimo

And I think over again
My small adventures
When with a shore wind I drifted out
In my kayak
And thought I was in danger.
My fears,
Those I thought so big,
For all the vital things
I had to get and to reach.

And yet, there is only
One great thing,
The only thing:
To live to see in huts and on journeys
The great day that dawns,
And the light that fills the world.

Wind Song

Pima

Wind now commences to sing;
  Wind now commences to sing.
The land stretches before me,
  Before me stretches away.

Wind's house now is thundering.
  Wind's house now is thundering.
I go roaring over the land,
  The land covered with thunder.

Over the windy mountains;
  Over the windy mountains,
Came the myriad-legged wind;
  The wind came running hither.

The black Snake Wind came to me;
  The Black Snake Wind came to me,
Came and wrapped itself about,
  Came here running with its songs.

Swift Things Are Beautiful

Elizabeth Coatsworth

Swift things are beautiful:
Swallows and deer,
And lightning that falls
Bright-veined and clear,
Rivers and meteors,
Wind in the wheat,
The strong-withered horse,
The runner's sure feet.

And slow things are beautiful:
The closing of day,
The pause of the wave
That curves downward to spray,
The ember that crumbles,
The opening flower,
And the ox that moves on
In the quiet of power.

Sandinista Avioncitos

Lawrence Ferlinghetti

The little airplanes of the heart
with their brave little propellers
What can they do
against the winds of darkness
even as butterflies are beaten back
by hurricanes
yet do not die
They lie in wait wherever
they can hide and hang
their fine wings folded
and when the killer-wind dies
they flutter forth again
into the new-blown light
live as leaves

A Blessing

James Wright

Just off the highway to Rochester, Minnesota,
Twilight bounds softly forth on the grass.
And the eyes of those two Indian ponies
Darken with kindness.
They have come gladly out of the willows
To welcome my friend and me.
We step over the barbed wire into the pasture
Where they have been grazing all day, alone.
They ripple tensely, they can hardly contain their happiness
That we have come.
They bow shyly as wet swans. They love each other.
There is no loneliness like theirs.
At home once more,
They begin munching the young tufts of spring in the darkness.
I would like to hold the slenderer one in my arms,
For she has walked over to me
And nuzzled my left hand.
She is black and white,
Her mane falls wild on her forehead,
And the light breeze moves me to caress her long ear
That is delicate as the skin over a girl's wrist.
Suddenly I realize
That if I stepped out of my body I would break
Into blossom.

Player Piano

John Updike

My stick fingers click with a snicker
   As, chuckling, they knuckle the keys;
Light-footed, my steel feelers flicker
   And pluck from these keys melodies.

My paper can caper; abandon
   Is broadcast by dint of my din,
And no man or band has a hand in
   The tones I turn on from within.

At times I'm a jumble of rumbles,
   At others I'm light like the moon,
But never my numb plunker fumbles,
   Misstrums me, or tries a new tune.

A Pizza the Size of the Sun

Jack Prelutsky

I'm making a pizza the size of the sun,
a pizza that's sure to weigh more than a ton,
a pizza too massive to pick up and toss,
a pizza resplendent with oceans of sauce.

I'm topping my pizza with mountains of cheese,
with acres of peppers, pimentos, and peas,
with mushrooms, tomatoes, and sausage galore,
with every last olive they had at the store.

My pizza is sure to be one of a kind,
my pizza will leave other pizzas behind,
my pizza will be a delectable treat
that all who love pizza are welcome to eat.

The oven is hot, I believe it will take
a year and a half for my pizza to bake.
I hardly can wait till my pizza is done,
my wonderful pizza the size of the sun.

The Darker Side
"The winds of darkness"

Baseball Cards #1

Jim Daniels

One
of the 10,342 baseball cards in my parents' attic
sneezes in the darkness, remembers
sweaty hands.

He calls to me across hundreds of miles:
Remember me, Jake Wood, 1964, 2nd base,
    Detroit Tigers,
Series 2, No. 272?
He wants to stretch his legs, climb out
from between Wilbur Wood and the 4th Series
    Checklist
wants to outsail all the other cards
in a game of farthies, float down
on Jose Tartabull in a game of tops.
He wants to smell like fresh from the pack
wants to be perfumed again
with the pink smell of bubble gum.

Dressed Up

Langston Hughes

I had ma clothes cleaned
Just like new.
I put 'em on but
I still feels blue.

I bought a new hat,
Sho is fine,
But I wish I had back that
Old gal o' mine.

I got new shoes—
They don't hurt ma feet,
But I ain't got nobody
For to call me sweet.

The Question Mark

Gevorg Emin

Translated by Diane Der-Hevanesslan

Poor thing. Poor crippled measure
of punctuation. Who would know,
who could imagine you used to be
an exclamation point?
What force bent you over?
Age, time and the vices
of this century?
Did you not once evoke,
call out and stress?
But you got weary of it all,
got wise, and turned like this.

The Garden of a Child

Nirendranath Chakravarti

I entered the garden of my childhood days after
the storm had passed over. A gentle breeze was
blowing and the sky was blue. Seeing in the
undergrowth a bird that had come out of an egg
only a little while ago and had fallen down, I
put it back in its nest.
It all happened yesterday. Today I am a grown-up
man again, and I just can't put anything back in
its proper place.

From A Very Little Sphinx

Edna St. Vincent Millay

Come along in then, little girl!
   Or else stay out!
But in the open door she stands,
And bites her lip and twists her hands,
And stares upon me, trouble-eyed:
"Mother," she says, "I can't decide!
I can't decide!"

Lost

Carl Sandburg

Desolate and lone
All night long on the lake
Where fog trails and mist creeps,
The whistle of a boat
Calls and cries unendingly,
Like some lost child
In tears and trouble
Hunting the harbor's breast
And the harbor's eyes.

Footpath

Stella Ngatho

Path-let . . . leaving home, leading out,
Return my mother to me.
The sun is sinking and darkness coming,
Hens and cocks are already inside and babies drowsing,
Return my mother to me.
We do not have fire-wood and I have not seen the lantern,
There is no more food and the water has run out.
Path-let I pray you, return my mother to me.
Path of the hillocks, path of the small stones,
Path of slipperiness, path of the mud,
Return my mother to me.
Path of the papyrus, path of the rivers,
Path of the small forests, path of the reeds,
Return my mother to me.
Path that winds, path of the short-cut,
Over-trodden path, newly-made path,
Return my mother to me.
Path, I implore you, return my mother to me.
Path of the crossways, path that branches off,
Path of the stinging shrubs, path of the bridge,
Return my mother to me.
Path of the open, path of the valley,
Path of the steep climb, path of the downward slope,
Return my mother to me.
Children are drowsing about to sleep,
Darkness is coming and there is no fire-wood,
And I have not yet found the lantern:
Return my mother to me.

Self Reflection
"Who makes these changes?"

Dream Boogie

Langston Hughes

Good morning, daddy!
Ain't you heard
The boogie-woogie rumble
Of a dream deferred?

Listen closely:
You'll hear their feet
Beating out and beating out a—

*You think
It's a happy beat?*

Listen to it closely:
Ain't you heard
something underneath
like a—

What did I say?

Sure,
I'm happy!
Take it away!

*Hey, pop!
Re-bop!
Mop!*

Y-e-a-h!

Who Makes These Changes?

Jalāl al-Dīn Rūmī

Who makes these changes?
I shoot an arrow right.
It lands left.
I ride after a deer and find myself
chased by a hog.
I plot to get what I want
and end up in prison.
I dig pits to trap others
and fall in.

I should be suspicious
of what I want.

A Man Said to the Universe

Stephen Crane

A man said to the universe:
"Sir, I exist!"
"However," replied the universe,
"The fact has not created in me
A sense of obligation."

Reflective

A. R. Ammons

I found a
weed
that had a

mirror in it
and that
mirror

looked in at
a mirror
in

me that
had a
weed in it

Gratitude

Louise Glück

Do not think I am not grateful for your small
kindness to me.
I like small kindnesses.
In fact I actually prefer them to the more
substantial kindness, that is always eying you,
like a large animal on a rug,
until your whole life reduces
to nothing but waking up morning after morning
cramped, and the bright sun shining on its tusks.

Yield

Ronald Gross

Yield.
No Parking.
Unlawful to Pass.
Wait for Green Light.
Yield.

Stop.
Narrow Bridge.
Merging Traffic Ahead
Yield.

Yield.

The Secret Sits

Robert Frost

We dance round in a ring and suppose,
But the Secret sits in the middle and knows.

Forgive My Guilt

Robert P. Tristram Coffin

Not always sure what things called sins may be,
I am sure of one sin I have done.
It was years ago, and I was a boy,
I lay in the frostflowers with a gun,
The air ran blue as the flowers, I held my breath,
Two birds on golden legs slim as dream things
Ran like quicksilver on the golden sand,
My gun went off, they ran with broken wings.
Into the sea, I ran to fetch them in,
But they swam with their heads high out to sea,
They cried like two sorrowful high flutes,
With jagged ivory bones where wings should be.

For days I heard them when I walked that headland
Crying out to their kind in the blue,
The other plovers were going over south
On silver wings leaving these broken two.
The cries went out one day; but I still hear them
Over all the sounds of sorrow in war or peace
I ever have heard, time cannot drown them,
Those slender flutes of sorrow never cease.
Two airy things forever denied the air!
I never knew how their lives at last were spilt,
But I have hoped for years all that is wild,
Airy, and beautiful will forgive my guilt.

I May Live On Until

Fujiwara No Kiyosuke

I may live on until
I long for this time
In which I am so unhappy,
And remember it fondly.

prayer

lucille clifton

lighten up

why is your hand
so heavy
on just poor
me?

answer

this is the stuff
i made the heroes
out of
all the saints
and prophets and things
had to come by
this

The Span of Life

Robert Frost

The old dog barks backward without getting up.
I can remember when he was a pup.

Interlude III

Karl Shapiro

Writing, I crushed an insect with my nail
And thought nothing at all. A bit of wing
Caught my eye then, a gossamer so frail

An exquisite, I saw in it a thing
That scorned the grossness of the thing I wrote.
It hung upon my finger like a sting.

A leg I noticed next, fine as a mote,
"And on this frail eyelash he walked," I said,
"And climbed and walked like any mountain-goat."

And in this mood I sought the little head,
But it was lost; then in my heart a fear
Cried out, "A life—why beautiful, why dead!"

It was a mite that held itself most dear,
So small I could have drowned it with a tear.

I'm Drifting
Through Negative Space

Jack Prelutsky

I'm drifting through negative space,
a frown on my lack of a face,
attempting to hear
with a tenuous ear
what nobody says in this place.
Undressed in unknowable clothes,
I strike an impossible pose,
then rest my non-head
on my shadowy bed,
and when I awaken, I doze.

I'm eating a make-believe bite,
today in the negative night.
The water I drink
from my fictional sink
is dry as the darkness is light.
I toss an ephemeral ball
against an impalpable wall.
It bounces and lands
in my vanishing hands—
it's hard to keep track of it all.

I'd like to be positive, but
I'm stuck in a negative rut.
I laugh when I'm sad,
when I'm angry, I'm glad,
whatever I open, I shut.
I'm running an opposite race,
maintaining an imprecise pace.
I lose when I win,
going out coming in—
it's eerie in negative space.

Lineage

Margaret Walker

My grandmothers were strong.
They followed plows and bent to toil.
The moved through fields sowing seed.
The touched earth and grain grew.
They were full of sturdiness and singing.
My grandmothers were strong.

My grandmothers are full of memories.
Smelling of soap and onions and wet clay.
With veins rolling roughly over quick hands.
They have many clean words to say.
My grandmothers were strong.
Why am I not as they?

Reflecting on Others "Have I learned to understand you?"

You Say, "I Will Come"

Lady Ōtomo No Sakanoe

Translated by Kenneth Rexroth

You say, "I will come."
And you do not come.
Now you say, "I will not come."
So I shall expect you.
Have I learned to understand you?

Patrick Ewing Takes a Foul Shot

Diane Ackerman

Ewing sweating,
molding the ball
with spidery hands,
packing it, packing it,
into a snowball's
chance of a goal,
rolling his shoulders
through a silent earthquake,
rocking from one foot
to the other, sweating,
bouncing it, oh, sweet
honey, molding it,
packing it tight,
he fires:

floats it up on one palm
as if surfacing
from the clear green Caribbean
with a shell
whose roar wraps around him,
whose surf breaks
deep into his arena
where light and time
and pupils jump
because he jumps

Foul Shot

Edwin A. Hoey

With two 60's stuck on the scoreboard
And two seconds hanging on the clock,
The solemn boy in the center of eyes,
Squeezed by silence,
Seeks out the line with his feet,
Soothes his hands along his uniform,
Gently drums the ball against the floor,
Then measures the waiting net,
Raises the ball on his right hand,
Balances it with his left,
Calms it with fingertips,
Breathes,
Crouches,
Waits,
And then through a stretching of stillness,
Nudges it upward.

The ball
Slides up and out,
Lands,
Leans,
Wobbles,
Wavers,
Hesitates,
Exasperates,
Plays it coy
Until every face begs with unsounding screams—
And then

        And then

                And then,

Right before ROAR-UP,
Dives down and through.

Analysis of Baseball

May Swenson

It's about
the ball,
the bat,
and the mitt.
Ball hits
bat, or it
hits mitt.
Bat doesn't
hit ball, bat
meets it.
Ball bounces
off bat, flies
air, or thuds
ground (dud)
or it
fits mitt.

Bat waits
for ball
to mate.
Ball hates
to take bat's
bait. Ball
flirts, bat's
late, don't
keep the date.
Ball goes in
(thwack) to mitt,
and goes out
(thwack) back
to mitt.

Ball fits
mitt, but
not all
the time.
Sometimes
ball gets hit
(pow) when bat
meets it,
and sails
to a place
where mitt
has to quit
in disgrace.
That's about
the bases
loaded,
about 40,000
fans exploded.

It's about
the ball,
the bat,
the mitt,
the bases
and the fans.
It's done
on a diamond,
and for fun.
It's about
home, and it's
about run.

To Satch[1]

Samuel Allen (Paul Vesey)

Sometimes I feel like I will *never* stop
dust go on forever
Till one fine mornin'
I'm gonna reach up and grab me a handfulla stars
Swing out my long lean leg
And whip three hot strikes burnin' down the heavens
And look over at God and say
How about that!

1. **Satch:** LeRoy Robert "Satchell" Paige, the legendary black baseball pitcher
   (1905–1982) played for more than 20 years in the Negro leagues. Upon the deseg-
   regation of baseball, he entered the major leagues in 1948 where, despite his
   advanced age, he helped the Cleveland Indians to a World Series championship.

In Memoriam John Coltrane

Michael Stillman

Listen to the coal
rolling, rolling through the cold
steady rain, wheel on

wheel, listen to the
turning of the wheels this night
black as coal dust, steel

on steel, listen to
these cars carry coal, listen
to the coal train roll.

Eleanor Rigby

John Lennon and Paul McCartney

Ah, look at all the lonely people!
Ah, look at all the lonely people!

Eleanor Rigby
Picks up the rice in the church where a wedding has been,
Lives in a dream,
Waits at the window
Wearing the face that she keeps in a jar by the door.
Who is it for?

All the lonely people,
Where do they all come from?
All the lonely people,
Where do they all belong?

Father McKenzie,
Writing the words of a sermon that no one will hear,
No one comes near
Look at him working,
Darning his socks in the night when there's nobody there.
What does he care?

All the lonely people
Where do they all come from?
All the lonely people
Where do they all belong?

Eleanor Rigby
Died in the church and was buried along with her name.
Nobody came.
Father McKenzie,
Wiping the dirt from his hands as he walks from the grave,
No one was saved.

All the lonely people,
Where do they all come from?
All the lonely people,
Where do they all belong?

Ah, look at all the lonely people!
Ah, look at all the lonely people!

Chocolates

Louis Simpson

Once some people were visiting Chekhov.
While they made remarks about his genius
the Master fidgeted. Finally
he said, "Do you like chocolates?"

They were astonished, and silent.
He repeated the question,
whereupon one lady plucked up her courage
and murmured shyly, "Yes."

"Tell me," he said, leaning forward,
light glinting from his spectacles,
"what kind? The light, sweet chocolate
or the dark, bitter kind?"

The conversation became general.
They spoke of cherry centers,
of almonds and Brazil nuts.
Losing their inhibitions
they interrupted one another.
For people may not know what they think
about politics in the Balkans,
or the vexed question of men and women,

but everyone has a definite opinion
about the flavor of shredded coconut.
Finally someone spoke of chocolates filled with liqueur,
and everyone, even the author of *Uncle Vanya*,
was at a loss for words.

As they were leaving he stood by the door
and took their hands.
                    In the coach returning to Petersburg
they agreed that it had been a most
unusual conversation.

Mama Is a Sunrise

Evelyn Tooley Hunt

When she comes slip-footing through the door,
   she kindles us
   like lump coal lighted,
   and we wake up glowing.
She puts a spark even in Papa's eyes
and turns out all our darkness.

When she comes sweet-talking in the room,
   she warms us
   like grits and gravy,
   and we rise up shining.
Even at night-time Mama is a sunrise
that promises tomorrow and tomorrow.

Moments in Time
"This could go on forever"

Far and Close

Gu Cheng

Translated by Edward Morin

You
Look a while at me,
Look a while at a cloud.

I feel
You are far away while looking at me,
So very close while looking at the cloud.

The lightning flashes . . .

Matsuo Bashō

The lightning flashes
and slashing through the darkness,
 A night-heron's screech.

A lightning gleam

Matsuo Bashō

A lightning gleam:
 into the darkness travels
 a night heron's scream.

Fallen flowers rise

Moritake

Fallen flowers rise
  back to the branch—I watch:
    oh . . . butterflies!

The Open Shutter

Karl Krolow

Translated by Kevin Perryman

Someone pouring light
Out of the window.
The roses of air
Open.
And children
Playing in the street
Look up.
Pigeons nibble
At its sweetness.
Girls are beautiful
And men gentle
In this light.
But before the others say so
Someone shuts
The window again.

M. Degas Teaches Art & Science at Durfee Intermediate School

Philip Levine

He made a line on the blackboard,
one bold stroke from right to left
diagonally downward and stood back
to ask, looking as always at no one
in particular, "What have I done?"
From the back of the room Freddie
shouted, "You've broken a piece
of chalk." M. Degas did not smile.
"What have I done?" he repeated.
The most intellectual students
looked down to study their desks
except for Gertrude Bimmler, who raised
her hand before she spoke. "M. Degas,
you have created the hypotenuse
of an isosceles triangle." Degas mused.
Everyone knew that Gertrude could not
be incorrect. "It is possible,"
Louis Warshowsky added precisely,
"that you have begun to represent
the roof of a barn." I remember
that it was exactly twenty minutes
past eleven, and I thought at worst
this would go on another forty
minutes. It was early April,
the snow had all but melted on
the playgrounds, the elms and maples
bordering the cracked walks shivered
in the new winds, and I believed
that before I knew it I'd be
swaggering to the candy store
for a Milky Way. M. Degas
pursed his lips, and the room

stilled until the long hand
of the clock moved to twenty one
as though in complicity with Gertrude,
who added confidently, "You've begun
to separate the dark from the dark."
I looked back for help, but now
the trees bucked and quaked, and I
knew this could go on forever.

I Ask My Mother to Sing

Li-Young Lee

She begins, and my grandmother joins her.
Mother and daughter sing like young girls.
If my father were alive, he would play
his accordion and sway like a boat.

I've never been in Peking, or the Summer Palace,
nor stood on the great Stone Boat to watch
the rain begin on Kuen Ming Lake, the picnickers
running away in the grass.

But I love to hear it sung;
how the waterlilies fill with rain until
they overturn, spilling water into water,
then rock back, and fill with more.

Both women have begun to cry.
But neither stops her song.

Love
"Very fine is my Valentine"

Oh, My Love is Like a Red, Red Rose

Robert Burns

Oh, my love is like a red, red rose
    That's newly sprung in June;
My love is like the melody
    That's sweetly played in tune.

So fair art thou, my bonny lass,
    So deep in love am I;
And I will love thee still, my dear,
    Till a' the seas gang dry.

Till a' the seas gang dry, my dear,
    And the rocks melt wi' the sun;
And I will love thee still, my dear,
    While the sands o' life shall run.

And fare thee weel, my only love!
    And fare thee weel awhile!
And I will come again, my love
    Though it were ten thousand mile.

A Very Valentine

Gertrude Stein

Very fine is my valentine.
Very fine and very mine.
Very mine is my valentine very mine and very fine.
Very fine is my valentine and mine, very fine very
    mine and mine is my valentine.

Unfortunate Coincidence

Dorothy Parker

By the time you swear you're his,
　　Shivering and sighing,
And he vows his passion is
　　Infinite, undying—
Lady, make a note of this:
　　One of you is lying.

Everything Promised Him to Me

Anna Akhmatova

Everything promised him to me:
the fading amber edge of the sky,
and the sweet dreams of Christmas,
and the wind at Easter, loud with bells,

and the red shoots of the grapevine,
and waterfalls in the park,
and two large dragonflies
on the rusty iron fencepost.

And I could only believe
that he would be mine
as I walked along the high slopes,
the path of burning stones.

Natural History

E. B. White

The spider, dropping down from twig,
Unwinds a thread of her devising:
A thin, premeditated rig
To use in rising.

And all the journey down through space,
In cool descent, and loyal-hearted,
She builds a ladder to the place
From which she started.

Thus I, gone forth, as spiders do,
In spider's web a truth discerning,
Attach one silken strand to you
For my returning.

When, in Disgrace with fortune and men's eyes

William Shakespeare

When, in disgrace with Fortune and men's eyes,
I all alone beweep my outcast state,
And trouble deaf heaven with my bootless cries,
And look upon myself and curse my fate,
Wishing me like to one more rich in hope,
Featured like him, like him with friends possessed,
Desiring this man's art, and that man's scope,
With what I most enjoy contented least,
Yet in these thoughts myself almost despising,
Haply I think on thee, and then my state,
Like to the lark at break of day arising
From sullen earth, sings hymns at heaven's gate;
    For thy sweet love rememb'red such wealth brings
    That then I scorn to change my state with kings.

I think of the days . . .

Fujiwara No Atsutada

I think of the days
Before I met her
When I seemed to have
No troubles at all.

I Have Loved Hours at Sea

Sara Teasdale

I have loved hours at sea, gray cities,
   The fragile secret of a flower,
Music, the making of a poem
   That gave me heaven for an hour;

First stars above a snowy hill,
   Voices of people kindly and wise,
And the great look of love, long hidden,
   Found at last in meeting eyes.

New Love

Eve Merriam

I am telling my hands
not to blossom into roses

I am telling my feet
not to turn into birds
and fly over rooftops

and I am putting a hat on my head
so the flaming meteors
in my hair
will hardly show.

Conflict
"Let there be new flowering"

A Poison Tree

William Blake

I was angry with my friend:
I told my wrath, my wrath did end.
I was angry with my foe:
I told it not, my wrath did grow.

And I watered it in fears,
Night and morning with my tears;
And I sunned it with smiles,
And with soft deceitful wiles.

And it grew both day and night
Till it bore an apple bright;
And my foe beheld it shine,
And he knew that it was mine,

And into my garden stole
When the night had veiled the pole:
In the morning glad I see
My foe outstretched beneath the tree.

Ancient History

Arthur Guiterman

I hope the old Romans
Had painful abdomens.

I hope that the Greeks
Had toothache for weeks.

I hope the Egyptians
Had chronic conniptions.

I hope that the Arabs
Were bitten by scarabs.

I hope that the Vandals
Had thorns in their sandals.

I hope that the Persians
Had gout in all versions.

I hope that the Medes
Were kicked by their steeds.

They started the fuss
And left it to us!

Earth

John Hall Wheelock

"A planet doesn't explode of itself," said drily
The Martian astronomer, gazing off into the air—
"That they were able to do it is proof that highly
Intelligent beings must have been living there."

First Grade

William Stafford

In the play Amy didn't want to be
anybody; so she managed the curtain.
Sharon wanted to be Amy. But Sam
wouldn't let anybody be anybody else—
he said it was wrong. "All right," Steve said,
"I'll be me but I don't like it."
So Amy was Amy, and we didn't have the play.
And Sharon cried.

let there be new flowering

lucille clifton

let there be new flowering
in the fields let the fields
turn mellow for the men
let the men keep tender
through the time let the time
be wrested from the war
let the war be won
let love be
at the end

Washington Monument By Night

Carl Sandburg

The stone goes straight.
A lean swimmer dives into night sky,
Into half-moon mist.

Two trees are coal black.
This is a great white ghost between.
It is cool to look at.
Strong men, strong women, come here.

Eight years is a long time
To be fighting all the time.

The republic is a dream.
Nothing happens unless first a dream.

The wind bit hard at Valley Forge one Christmas.
Soldiers tied rags on their feet.
Red footprints wrote on the snow . . .
. . . and stone shoots into stars here
. . . into half-moon mist tonight.

Tongues wrangled dark at a man.
He buttoned his overcoat and stood alone.
In a snowstorm, red hollyberries, thoughts,
    he stood alone.

Napoleon

Miroslav Holub

Translated by Kaca Polackova

Children, when was
Napoleon Bonaparte
born? asks the teacher.

A thousand years ago, say the children.
A hundred years ago, say the children.
Nobody knows.

Children, what did
Napoleon Bonaparte
do? asks the teacher.

He won a war, say the children.
He lost a war, say the children.
Nobody knows.

Our butcher used to have a dog,
says Frankie,
and his name was Napoleon,
and the butcher used to beat him,
and the dog died
of hunger
a year ago.

And now all the children feel sorry
for Napoleon.

Sir, You Are Tough

Joseph Brodsky

Sir, you are tough, and I am tough.
But who will write whose epitaph?

Jerusalem

Yehuda Amichai

Translated by Stephen Mitchell

On a roof in the Old City
laundry hanging in the late afternoon sunlight:
the white sheet of a woman who is my enemy,
the towel of a man who is my enemy,
to wipe off the sweat of his brow.

In the sky of the Old City
a kite.
At the other end of the string,
a child
I can't see
because of the wall.

We have put up many flags,
they have put up many flags.
To make us think that they're happy.
To make them think that we're happy.

Overheard on a Saltmarsh

Harold Monro

Nymph, nymph, what are your beads?

Green glass, goblin. Why do you stare at them?

Give them me.

        No.

Give them me. Give them me.

            No.

Then I will howl all night in the reeds,
Lie in the mud and howl for them.

Goblin, why do you love them so?

They are better than stars or water,
Better than voices of winds that sing,
Better than any man's fair daughter,
Your green glass beads on a silver ring.

Hush, I stole them out of the moon.

Give me your beads, I want them.

                No.

I will howl in a deep lagoon
For your green glass beads, I love them so.
Give them me. Give them.

        No.

On a Sunny Evening

the children in Barracks L318 and L417
Terezín Concentration Camp, 1944

On a purple, sun-shot evening
Under wide-flowering chestnut trees
Upon the threshold full of dust
Yesterday, today, the days are all like these.

Trees flower forth in beauty,
Lovely too their very wood all gnarled and old
That I am half afraid to peer
Into their crowns of green and gold.

The sun has made a veil of gold
So lovely that my body aches.
Above, the heavens shriek with blue
Convinced I've smiled by some mistake.
The world's abloom and seems to smile.
I want to fly but where, how high?
If in barbed wire, things can bloom
Why couldn't I? I will not die!

Fear

Charles Simic

Fear passes from man to man
Unknowing,
As one leaf passes its shudder
To another.

All at once the whole tree is trembling
And there is no sign of the wind.

Animals
"We who dance hungry and wild"

The Lame Goat

Jalāl al-Dīn Rūmī

You've seen a herd of goats
going down to the water.

The lame and dreamy goat
brings up the rear.

There are worried faces about that one,
but now they're laughing,

because look, as they return,
that goat is leading!

There are many different kinds of knowing.
The lame goat's kind is a branch
that traces back to the roots of presence.

Learn from the lame goat,
and lead the herd home.

Monkeys

Klara Koettner-Benigni

Translated by Herbert Kuhner

The fact that we
don't understand
their language
doesn't mean
that they don't converse

If they could
understand us
they would
consider us to be
completely incomprehensible
and mad to boot

To a Squirrel at Kyle-na-no

William Butler Yeats

Come play with me.
Why should you run
Through the shaking tree
As though I'd a gun
To strike you dead?
When all I would do
Is to scratch your head
And let you go.

Six Variations (Part III)

Denise Levertov

Shlup, shlup, the dog
as it laps up
water
makes intelligent
music, resting
now and then to take breath in irregular
measure.

from

Ode to the Cat

Pablo Neruda

Translated by Ken Krabbenhoft

There was something wrong
with the animals:
their tails were too long, and they had
unfortunate heads.
Then they started coming together,
little by little
fitting together to make a landscape,
developing birthmarks, grace, pep.
But the cat,
only the cat
turned out finished,
and proud:
born in a state of total completion,
it sticks to itself and knows exactly what it wants.

The Sloth

Theodore Roethke

In moving slow he has no Peer.
You ask him something in his Ear,
He thinks about it for a Year;

And, then, before he says a Word
There, upside down (unlike a Bird),
He will assume that you have Heard—

A most Ex-as-per-at-ing Lug.
But should you call his manner Smug,
He'll sigh and give his Branch a Hug;

Then off again to Sleep he goes,
Still swaying gently by his Toes,
And you just *know* he knows he knows.

Buffalo Dusk

Carl Sandburg

The buffaloes are gone.
And those who saw the buffaloes are gone.
Those who saw the buffaloes by thousands and
    how they pawed the prairie sod into dust
    with their hoofs, their great heads down
    pawing on in a great pageant of dusk,
Those who saw the buffaloes are gone.
And the buffaloes are gone.

Mayflies

Paul Fleischman

Your Moment

Your hour

Your trifling day

We're mayflies
just emerging

rising from the river,
born this day in May

and dying day,

this single sip of living

We're mayflies
by the millions
fevered

rushed

We're mayflies
swarming, swerving,
rising high

courting on the wing,

We're mayflies
laying eggs
our final, frantic act.

light's weak

We're mayflies

Mayfly month

Mayfly year

Our life.
We're mayflies
just emerging

birthday

this particle of time

all that we're allowed.
We're mayflies
by the millions

frenzied

not redwood's centuries
to squander as we please.
We're mayflies
swarming, swerving,

then falling,

then mating in midair.
We're mayflies
laying eggs

Sun's low

in haste we launch them
down the stream.
We're mayflies

lying dying
floating by the millions

from which we sprung
so very long ago

back when we were
young.

lying dying

on the very stream

this morning
back when we were
young.

The Passenger Pigeon

Paul Fleischman

We were counted not in
    thousands
nor
    millions
but in
billions.
    billions.
    We were numerous as the

stars
    stars
    in the heavens
As grains of
sand
    sand
at the sea

    As the
buffalo
    buffalo
    on the plains.
When we burst into flight
    we so filled the sky
that the
sun
    sun
was darkened

    and
day
    day
    became dusk.
Humblers of the sun
    Humblers of the sun
we were!
    we were!
The world
inconceivable
    inconceivable
    without us.

Yet it's 1914,
and here I am
alone
    alone
    caged in the Cincinnati Zoo.

the last
    of the passenger pigeons.

The Firefly

Li Tai Po

I think
if you flew
up to the sky
beside the moon,
you would
twinkle
like a star.

The Rum Tum Tugger

T. S. Eliot

The Rum Tum Tugger is a Curious Cat:
If you offer him pheasant he would rather have grouse.
If you put him in a house he would much prefer a flat,
If you put him in a flat then he'd rather have a house.
If you set him on a mouse then he only wants a rat,
If you set him on a rat then he'd rather chase a mouse.
Yes the Rum Tum Tugger is a Curious Cat—
   And there isn't any call for me to shout it:
      For he will do
      As he do do
         And there's no doing anything about it!

   The Rum Tum Tugger is a terrible bore:
When you let him in, then he wants to be out;
He's always on the wrong side of every door,
And as soon as he's at home, then he'd like to get about.
He likes to lie in the bureau drawer,
But he makes such a fuss if he can't get out.
Yes the Rum Tum Tugger is a Curious Cat—
   And it isn't any use for you to doubt it:
      For he will do
      As he do do
         And there's no doing anything about it!

The Rum Tum Tugger is a curious beast:
His disobliging ways are a matter of habit.
If you offer him fish then he always wants a feast;
When there isn't any fish then he won't eat rabbit.
If you offer him cream then he sniffs and sneers,
For he only likes what he finds for himself;
So you'll catch him in it right up to the ears,
If you put it away on the larder shelf.
The Rum Tum Tugger is artful and knowing,
The Rum Tum Tugger doesn't care for a cuddle;
But he'll leap on your lap in the middle of your sewing,
For there's nothing he enjoys like a horrible muddle.
Yes the Rum Tum Tugger is a Curious Cat—
   And there isn't any need for me to spout it:
     For he will do
     As he do do
       And there's no doing anything about it!

The Rabbits' Song Outside the Tavern

Elizabeth Coatsworth

We, who play under the pines,
We, who dance in the snow
That shines blue in the light of the moon,
Sometimes halt as we go—
Stand with our ears erect,
Our noses testing the air,
To gaze at the golden world
Behind the windows there.

Suns they have in a cave,
Stars, each on a tall white stem,
And the thought of a fox or an owl
Seems never to trouble them.
They laugh and eat and are warm,
Their food is ready at hand,
While hungry out in the cold
We little rabbits stand.

But they never dance as we dance!
They haven't the speed nor the grace.
We scorn both the dog and the cat
Who lie by their fireplace.
We scorn them licking their paws
Their eyes on an upraised spoon—
We who dance hungry and wild
Under a winter's moon.

Where did that dog . . .

Shimaki Akahiko

Where did that dog
that used to be here go?
I thought about him
once again tonight
before I went to bed.

Crows

David McCord

I like to walk
And hear the black crows talk.

I like to lie
And watch crows sail the sky.

I like the crow
That wants the wind to blow:

I like the one
That thinks the wind is fun.

I like to see
Crows spilling from a tree,

And try to find
The top crow left behind.

I like to hear
Crows caw that spring is near.

I like the great
Wild clamor of crow hate

Three farms away
When owls are out by day.

I like the slow
Tired homeward-flying crow;

I like the sight
Of crows for my good night.

The Cardinal
in
the
Birdbath

Gail Kredenser Mack

A cardinal stopped by the birdbath; and I at the sink where
dishes were waiting, watched from the kitchen window as
round the edge he hopped, as if to test the water
with a toe.
Bobbing his
bright
head,
he
drank
and
drank;
then
hopped in
with all abandon,
and
splashed
and
splashed
again, gaily,
like a
child.
Wings busily aflutter,
he showered
diamonds
sparkling
from his
scarlet
feathers
down upon
the myrtle;
Cleansed of worldly dust,
he flew, a ruby flash, high, high
into the dappled coolness of the nodding maple.
And he and I went about our work, both of us singing.

Summer
"I like hot days"

House of Spring

Musō Soseki

Translated by W. S. Merwin and Soiku Shigematsu

Hundreds of open flowers
    all come from
        the one branch
Look
    all their colors
        appear in my garden
I open the clattering gate
    and in the wind
        I see
the spring sunlight
    already it has reached
        worlds without number

Midsummer, Tobago

Derek Walcott

Broad sun-stoned beaches.

White heat.
A green river.

A bridge,
scorched yellow palms

from the summer-sleeping house
drowsing through August.

Days I have held,
days I have lost,

days that outgrow, like daughters,
my harbouring arms.

Summer

Walter Dean Myers

I like hot days, hot days
Sweat is what you got days
Bugs buzzin from cousin to cousin
Juices dripping
Running and ripping
Catch the one you love days

Birds peeping
Old men sleeping
Lazy days, daisies lay
Beaming and dreaming
Of hot days, hot days,
Sweat is what you got days

Knoxville, Tennessee

Nikki Giovanni

I always like summer
best
you can eat fresh corn
from daddy's garden
and okra
and greens
and cabbage
and lots of
barbecue
and buttermilk
and homemade ice-cream
at the church picnic
and listen to
gospel music
outside
at the church
homecoming
and go to the mountains with
your grandmother
and go barefooted
and be warm
all the time
not only when you go to bed
and sleep

Winter
"Once a snowflake fell"

Splinter

Carl Sandburg

The voice of the last cricket
across the first frost
is one kind of good-by.
It is so thin a splinter of singing.

When It Is Snowing

Siv Cedering

When it is snowing
the blue jay
is the only piece of
sky
in my
backyard.

Revival

Steve Crow

Snow is a mind
falling, a continuous breath
of climbs, loops, spirals,
dips into the earth
like white fireflies
wanting to land, finding
a wind between houses,
diving like moths
into their own light
so that one wonders
if snow is a wing's
long memory across winter.

Preludes

T. S. Eliot

I

The winter evening settles down
With smell of steaks in passageways.
Six o'clock.
The burnt-out ends of smoky days.
And now a gusty shower wraps
The grimy scraps
Of withered leaves about your feet
And newspapers from vacant lots;
The showers beat
On broken blinds and chimney-pots,
And at the corner of the street
A lonely cab-horse steams and stamps.
And then the lighting of the lamps.

II

The morning comes to consciousness
Of faint stale smells of beer
From the sawdust-trampled street
With all its muddy feet that press
To early coffee-stands.
With the other masquerades
That time resumes,
One thinks of all the hands
That are raising dingy shades
In a thousand furnished rooms.

III

You tossed a blanket from the bed,
You lay upon your back, and waited;
You dozed, and watched the night revealing
The thousand sordid images
Of which your soul was constituted;
They flickered against the ceiling.
And when all the world came back
And the light crept up between the shutters
And you heard the sparrows in the gutters,

You had such a vision of the street
As the street hardly understands;
Sitting along the bed's edge, where
You curled the papers from your hair,
Or clasped the yellow soles of feet
In the palms of both soiled hands.

IV

His soul stretched tight across the skies
That fade behind a city block,
Or trampled by insistent feet
At four and five and six o'clock;
And short square fingers stuffing pipes,
And evening newspapers, and eyes
Assured of certain certainties,
The conscience of a blackened street
Impatient to assume the world.

I am moved by fancies that are curled
Around these images, and cling:
The notion of some infinitely gentle
Infinitely suffering thing.

Wipe your hand across your mouth, and laugh;
The worlds revolve like ancient women
Gathering fuel in vacant lots.

Too Much Snow

Louis Jenkins

Unlike the Eskimos we only have one word for snow but we have a lot of modifiers for that word. There is too much snow, which, unlike rain, does not immediately run off. It falls and stays for months. Someone wished for this snow. Someone got a deal, five cents on the dollar, and spent the entire family fortune. It's the simple solution, it covers everything. We are never satisfied with the arrangement of the snow so we spend hours moving the snow from one place to another. Too much snow. I box it up and send it to family and friends. I send a big box to my cousin in California. I send a small box to my mother. She writes "Don't send so much. I'm all alone now. I'll never be able to use so much." To you I send a single snowflake, beautiful, complex and delicate; different from all the others.

The Moon's the
North Wind's Cooky
(What the little girl said)

Vachel Lindsay

The Moon's the North Wind's cooky.
He bites it, day by day,
Until there's but a rim of scraps,
That crumble all away.

The South Wind is a baker.
He kneads clouds in his den,
And bakes a crisp new moon that . . . greedy
North . . . Wind . . . eats . . . again!

On a Night of Snow

Elizabeth Coatsworth

Cat, if you go outdoors you must walk in the snow.
You will come back with little white shoes on your feet,
Little white slippers of snow that have heels of sleet.
Stay by the fire, my Cat. Lie still, do not go.
See how the flames are leaping and hissing low.
I will bring you a saucer of milk like a marguerite,
So white and so smooth, so spherical and so sweet.
Stay with me, Cat. Outdoors the wild winds blow.

Outdoors the wild winds blow, Mistress, and dark is the night.
Strange voices cry in the trees, intoning strange lore,
And more than cats move, lit by our eyes' green light,
On silent feet where the meadow grasses hang hoar—
Mistress, there are portents abroad of magic and might,
And things that are yet to be done. Open the door!

Snow Toward Evening

Melville Cane

Suddenly the sky turned gray,
The day,
Which had been bitter and chill,
Grew soft and still.
Quietly
From some invisible blossoming tree
Millions of petals cool and white
Drifted and blew,
Lifted and flew,
Fell with the falling night.

Winter Scene

A. R. Ammons

There is now not a single
leaf on the cherry tree:

except when the jay
plummets in, lights, and,

in pure clarity, squalls:
then every branch

quivers and
breaks out in blue leaves.

Night
"The night has driven the shadow"

Window

Carl Sandburg

Night from a railroad care window
Is a great, dark, soft thing
Broken across with slashes of light.

When I Heard the Learn'd Astronomer

Walt Whitman

When I heard the learn'd astronomer,
When the proofs, the figures, were ranged in columns
   before me,
When I was shown the charts and diagrams, to add, divide,
   and measure them,
When I sitting heard the astronomer where he lectured
   with much applause in the lecture-room,
How soon unaccountable I became tired and sick,
Till rising and gliding out I wandered off by myself,
In the mystical moist night-air, and from time to time,
Looked up in perfect silence at the stars.

Acquainted with the Night

Robert Frost

I have been one acquainted with the night.
I have walked out in rain—and back in rain.
I have outwalked the furthest city light.

I have looked down the saddest city lane.
I have passed by the watchman on his beat
And dropped my eyes, unwilling to explain.

I have stood still and stopped the sound of feet
When far away an interrupted cry
Came over houses from another street,

But not to call me back or say good-by:
And further still at an unearthly height
One luminary clock against the sky

Proclaimed the time was neither wrong nor right.
I have been one acquainted with the night.

Night

Sara Teasdale

Stars over snow,
    And in the west a planet
Swinging below a star—
    Look for a lovely thing and you will find it,
It is not far—
    It never will be far.

The Falling Star

Sara Teasdale

I saw a star slide down the sky,
Blinding the north as it went by,
Too lovely to be bought or sold,
Too burning and too quick to hold,
Good only to make wishes on
And then forever to be gone.

who are you, little i

e. e. cummings

who are you, little i

(five or six years old)
peering from some high

window; at the gold

of november sunset

(and feeling: that if day
has to become night

this is a beautiful way)

Memory
"It seems like only yesterday"

My Father's Song

Simon Ortiz

Wanting to say things,
I miss my father tonight.
His voice, the slight catch,
the depth from his thin chest,
the tremble of emotion
in something he has just said
to his son, his song:

   We planted corn one Spring at Acu—
   we planted several times
   but this one particular time

On Turning Ten

Billy Collins

The whole idea of it makes me feel
like I'm coming down with something,
something worse than any stomach ache
or the headaches I get from reading in bad light—
a kind of measles of the spirit,
a mumps of the psyche,
a disfiguring chicken pox of the soul.

You tell me it is too early to be looking back,
but that is because you have forgotten
the perfect simplicity of being one
and the beautiful complexity introduced by two.
But I can lie on my bed and remember every digit.
At four I was an Arabian wizard.
I could make myself invisible
by drinking a glass of milk a certain way.
At seven I was a soldier, at nine a prince.

But now I am mostly at the window
watching the late afternoon light.
Back then it never fell so solemnly
against the side of my tree house,
and my bicycle never leaned against the garage
as it does today,
all the dark blue speed drained out of it.

This is the beginning of sadness, I say to myself,
as I walk through the universe in my sneakers.
It is time to say good-bye to my imaginary friends,
time to turn the first big number.
It seems only yesterday I used to believe
there was nothing under my skin but light.
If you cut me I would shine.
But now when I fall upon the sidewalks of life,
I skin my knees. I bleed.

Fortune

Lawrence Ferlinghetti

Fortune
    has its cookies to give out

which is a good thing

      since it's been a long time since

   that summer in Brooklyn
when they closed off the street
    one hot day
    and the

        FIREMEN

          turned on their hoses

and all the kids ran out in it

    in the middle of the street

  and there were

      maybe a couple dozen of us

         out there

with the water squirting up
      to the

     sky

      and all over
       us
  there was maybe only six of us
       kids altogether

running around in our
barefeet and birthday
suits
and I remember Molly but then

the firemen stopped squirting their hoses
all of a sudden and went
back in
their firehouse
and
started playing pinochle again
just as if nothing
had ever
happened
while I remember Molly
looked at me and

ran in

because I guess really we were the only ones there

First Day Back

Yuka Igarashi

My father went to Spain
And came home with
Jet lag
He said he couldn't sleep
At night
And that he was awfully tired
All day
And that he felt
Sort of blurry and
Sort of bewildered
Almost like he was floating
Somewhere
Well you know
I guess
School
And summer
Are in different time zones
Too

Deformed Finger

Hal Sirowitz

Don't stick your finger in the ketchup bottle,
Mother said. It might get stuck, &
then you'll have to wait for your father
to get home to pull it out. He
won't be happy to find a dirty fingernail
squirming in the ketchup that he's going to use
on his hamburger. He'll yank it out so hard
that for the rest of your life you won't
be able to wear a ring on that finger.
And if you ever get a girlfriend, &
you hold hands, she's bound to ask you
why one of your fingers is deformed,
& you'll be obligated to tell her how
you didn't listen to your mother, &
insisted on playing with a ketchup bottle,
& she'll get to thinking, he probably won't
listen to me either, & she'll push your hand away.

The Fury of Overshoes

Anne Sexton

They sit in a row
outside the kindergarten,
black, red, brown, all
with those brass buckles.
Remember when you couldn't
buckle your own
overshoe
or tie your own
shoe
or cut your own meat
and the tears
running down like mud
because you fell off your
tricycle?
Remember, big fish,
when you couldn't swim
and simply slipped under
like a stone frog?
The world wasn't
yours.

It belonged to
the big people.
Under your bed
sat the wolf
and he made a shadow
when cars passed by
at night.
They made you give up
your nightlight
and your teddy
and your thumb.
Oh, overshoes,
don't you
remember me,
pushing you up and down
in the winter snow?

Oh thumb,
I want a drink,
it is dark,
where are the big people,
when will I get there,
taking giant steps
all day,
each day
and thinking
nothing of it?

To a Daughter Leaving Home

Linda Pastan

When I taught you
at eight to ride
a bicycle, loping along
beside you
as you wobbled away
on two round wheels,
my own mouth rounding
in surprise when you pulled
ahead down the curved
path of the park,
I kept waiting
for the thud
of your crash as I
sprinted to catch up,
while you grew
smaller, more breakable
with distance,
pumping, pumping
for your life, screaming
with laughter,
the hair flapping
behind you like a
handkerchief waving
goodbye.

Creative Thoughts
"Finding new words"

Voice in the Crowd

Ted Joans

If you should see/a man/walking
   down a crowded street/talking aloud/to himself
    don't run/in the opposite direction
     but run toward him/for he is a *poet!*

    You have nothing to fear/from the poet
    but the truth

The Pen

Muhammad al-Ghuzzi

Translated by May Jayyusi and John Heath-Stubbs

Take a pen in your uncertain fingers
Trust, and be assured
That the whole world is a sky-blue butterfly
And words are the nets to capture it.

On Reading Poems to a Senior Class at South High

D. C. Berry

Before
I opened my mouth
I noticed them sitting there
as orderly as frozen fish
in a package.

Slowly water began to fill the room
though I did not notice it
till it reached
my ears

and then I heard the sounds
of fish in an aquarium

and I knew that though I had
tried to drown them
with my words
that they had only opened up
like gills for them
and let me in.

Together we swam around the room
like thirty tails whacking words
till the bell rang
puncturing
a hole in the door

where we all leaked out

They went to another class
I suppose and I home

At the Beach

Kemal Ozer

Translated by O. Yalim, W. Fielder, and Dionis Riggs

The waves are erasing the footprints
Of those who are walking the beach

The wind is carrying away the words
Two people are saying to each other

But still they are walking the beach
Their feet making new footprints

Still the two are talking together
Finding new words.

Unfolding Bud

Naoshi Koriyama

One is amazed
By a water-lily bud
Unfolding
With each passing day,
Taking on a richer color
And new dimensions.

One is not amazed,
At a first glance,
By a poem,
Which is as tight-closed
As a tiny bud.

Yet one is surprised
To see the poem
Gradually unfolding,
Revealing its rich inner self,
As one reads it
Again
And over again.

How to Eat a Poem

Eve Merriam

Don't be polite.
Bite in.
Pick it up with your fingers and lick the juice
    that may run down your chin.
It is ready and ripe now, whenever you are.
You do not need a knife or fork or spoon
or plate or napkin or tablecloth.
For there is no core
or stem
or rind
or pit
or seed
or skin
to throw away.

Autobiographia Literaria

Frank O'Hara

When I was a child
I played by myself in a
corner of the schoolyard
all alone.

I hated dolls and I
hated games, animals were
not friendly and birds
flew away.

If anyone was looking
for me I hid behind a
tree and cried out "I am
an orphan."

And here I am, the
center of all beauty!
writing these poems!
Imagine!

The Secret

Denise Levertov

Two girls discover
the secret of life
in a sudden line of
poetry.

I who don't know the
secret wrote
the line. They
told me

(through a third person)
they had found it
but not what it was
not even

what line it was. No doubt
by now, more than a week
later, they have forgotten
the secret,

the line, the name of
the poem. I love them
for finding what
I can't find,

and for loving me
for the line I wrote,
and for forgetting it
so that

a thousand times, till death
finds them, they may
discover it again, in other
lines

in other
happenings. And for
wanting to know it,
for

assuming there is
such a secret, yes,
for that
most of all.

Funny Stuff
"It's gone off its rocker today"

Invisible Cat

X. J. Kennedy

One day Snow Leopard caught a cough
And sneezed so hard his spots fell off.

Now every time it starts in snowing,
Don't look for him. He won't be showing.

Only one guy and . . .

Kobayashi Issa

Translated by Cid Corman

only one guy and
only one fly trying to
make the guest room do

A Handful of Limericks

Anonymous

I sat next the Duchess at tea.
It was just as I feared it would be:
    Her rumblings abdominal
    Were simply abominable,
And everyone thought it was me.

There was a young lady of Lynn
Who was so uncommonly thin
    That when she essayed
    To drink lemonade
She slipped through the straw and fell in.

A tutor who tooted the flute
Tried to tutor two tooters to toot.
   Said the two to the tutor,
   "Is it harder to toot or
To tutor two tooters to toot?"

There was a young maid who said, "Why
Can't I look in my ear with my eye?
   If I put my mind to it,
   I'm sure I can do it.
You never can tell till you try."

There was an old man of Peru
Who dreamt he was eating his shoe.
   He awoke in the night
   In a terrible fright,
And found it was perfectly true!

A decrepit old gas man named Peter,
While hunting around for the meter,
   Touched a leak with his light.
   He arose out of sight,
And, as anyone can see by reading this, he
     also destroyed the meter.

Well, it's partly the shape of the thing
That gives the old limerick wing;
   These accordion pleats
   Full of airy conceits
Take it up like a kite on a string.

Parking Lot Full

Eve Merriam

a much of motors
an over of drives
a choke of carburetors
a flood of engines
a plethora of wheels
a googol of gas tanks
a total of exhausts

Eletelephony

Laura E. Richards

Once there was an elephant,
Who tried to use the telephant—
No! No! I mean an elephone
Who tried to use the telephone—
(Dear me! I am not certain quite
That even now I've got it right.)

Howe'er it was, he got his trunk
Entangled in the telephunk;
The more he tried to get it free,
The louder buzzed the telephee—
(I fear I'd better drop the song
Of elephop and telephong!)

The Octopus

Ogden Nash

Tell me, O Octopus, I begs,
Is those things arms, or is they legs?
I marvel at thee, Octopus;
If I were thou, I'd call me Us.

A Caution to Everybody

Ogden Nash

Consider the auk;
Becoming extinct because he forgot how to fly, and could
    only walk.
Consider man, who may well become extinct
Because he forgot how to walk and learned how to fly
    before he thinked.

Said a Long Crocodile

Lilian Moore

Said a very l—o—n—g crocodile,
"My length is a terrible trial!
    I know I should diet
    But each time I try it
I'm hungry for more than a mile!"

The Vulture

Hilaire Belloc

The vulture eats between his meals,
    And that's the reason why
He very, very rarely feels
    As well as you and I.
His eye is dull, his head is bald,
    His neck is growing thinner.
Oh! what a lesson for us all
    To only eat at dinner!

I Think My Computer is Crazy

Jack Prelutsky

I think my computer is crazy,
it's gone off its rocker today,
the screen is impossibly scrambled,
and I can't control the display.
Illegible symbols are flashing
in places they just don't belong,
it's surely no help with my homework,
every last answer is wrong.

I'd always depended upon it,
but now its behavior has changed,
it's churning out absolute drivel,
it's clear my computer's deranged.
It's making disheartening noises,
like kangaroos hopping on fruit,
it thoroughly garbles my input,
then burbles, **"THIS DOES NOT COMPUTE!"**

Something inside my computer
is buzzing like billions of bees,
even my mouse is affected,
it seems to be begging for cheese.
I guess I know why my computer
is addled and may not survive—
my brother inserted bologna
into the floppy disk drive.

The Goops

Gelett Burgess

The Goops they lick their fingers,
   And the Goops they lick their knives;
They spill their broth on the tablecloth—
   Oh, they lead disgusting lives!
The Goops they talk while eating,
   And loud and fast they chew;
And that is why I'm glad that I
   Am not a Goop—are you?

Ponder This
"I am puzzled"

Oh No

Robert Creeley

If you wander far enough
you will come to it
and when you get there
they will give you a place to sit

for yourself only, in a nice chair,
and all your friends will be there
with smiles on their faces
and they will likewise all have places.

Silence

Marianne Moore

My father used to say,
"Superior people never make long visits,
have to be shown Longfellow's grave
or the glass flowers at Harvard.
Self-reliant like the cat—
that takes its prey to privacy,
the mouse's limp tail hanging like a shoelace from its mouth—
they sometimes enjoy solitude,
and can be robbed of speech
by speech which has delighted them.
The deepest feeling always shows itself in silence;
not in silence, but restraint."
Nor was he insincere in saying, "Make my house your inn."
Inns are not residences.

breaklight

lucille clifton

light keeps on breaking.
i keep knowing
the language of other nations.
i keep hearing
tree talk
water words
and i keep knowing what they mean.
and light just keeps on breaking.
last night
that fears of my mother came
knocking and when i
opened the door
they tried to explain themselves
and i understood
everything they said.

Meditatio

Ezra Pound

When I carefully consider the curious habits of dogs
I am compelled to conclude
That man is the superior animal.

When I consider the curious habits of man
I confess, my friend, I am puzzled.

What is it that upsets the volcanoes . . .

Pablo Neruda

Translated by William O'Daly

What is it that upsets the volcanoes
that spit fire, cold and rage?

Why wasn't Christopher Columbus
able to discover Spain?

How many questions does a cat have?

Do tears not yet spilled
wait in small lakes?

Or are they invisible rivers
that run toward sadness?

The Wounded Breakfast

Russell Edson

A huge shoe mounts up from the horizon, squealing and grinding forward on small wheels, even as a man sitting to breakfast on his veranda is suddenly engulfed in a great shadow, almost the size of the night.

He looks up and sees a huge shoe ponderously mounting out of the earth.

Up in the unlaced ankle-part an old woman stands at a helm behind the great tongue curled forward; the thick laces dragging like ships' rope on the ground as the huge thing squeals and grinds forward; children everywhere, they look from the shoelace holes, they crowd about the old woman, even as she pilots this huge shoe over the earth . . .

Soon the huge shoe is descending the opposite horizon, a monstrous snail squealing and grinding into the earth . . .

The man turns to his breakfast again, but sees it's been wounded, the yolk of one of his eggs is bleeding . . .

Just People

Kathi Appelt

At Mirabeau B. Lamar High School
　　there were plenty of heroes.

There was Jonathan Thomas—quarterback sensation
Ashley Riggerio—head cheerleader
Deanna Braden—Miss Teen Texas.
Sandy Hampton—whiz bang math genius.
The glamour crowd.

Certainly Marsha Cates—last chair French horn player
in the marching band—wasn't one of them.
And neither was her boyfriend Collie Simms—
　　Just an average student.
They went unnoticed by most, by teachers,
especially by the heroes.

But Collie didn't go unnoticed by Marsha
who knew about his love for poetry and wild animals.
And Marsha didn't go unnoticed by Collie
who knew about her soft laughter
and her secret affection for science fiction movies.
And maybe that's why they loved each other so
and why they were so quiet about it, their love.
Because they weren't heroes—
just people, loving.
At Mirabeau B. Lamar everyone's attention was on
which hero liked which hero.
No one really knew about Marsha Cates
and Collie Sims and their love for each other.
No one really cared.

Except perhaps a few in the French horn section.

So when Collie was hit by a drunken driver
one warm spring night on his way home from Marsha's,
where they had talked about arctic foxes
and watched *Close Encounters of the Third Kind*

in the same evening, when Marsha had played that tune,
A-B-G-G-D in perfect whole notes on her French horn,
most people at Mirabeau B. Lamar
couldn't even picture his face
    when they closed their eyes

But not Marsha who couldn't *not* picture his face.

And weeks, even months later
    most people at Mirabeau B. Lamar
hadn't heard that Marsha still loved Collie
or even that she ever had.
Least of all the glamour crowd.

That didn't matter to Marsha.
She knew Collie didn't care about being
something he wasn't.

But she did know something about Collie and herself,
something shared, something pure
    and sweet and important.
It was just that she couldn't find the way to tell it.

She wanted to—
how important Collie's loving had been,
how that counted.

It drove her day and night
through home room
through band practice
through dinner at night
through her dreams.
But she couldn't find the way.

And only a few people in the French horn section
had the slightest idea that Marsha, so quiet
and unnoticed was coming undone.

So it figured that the French horn section knew first
when Marsha Cates stopped marching
    in the middle of the field
during half-time at the homecoming game.

She just stopped while the band marched around her
and left her there on the 43rd yard line
all alone facing the bleachers and all the heroes.
For a moment no one noticed
for Marsha Cates wasn't the noticed kind.
But then someone pointed to her,
    all alone on the 43rd yard line.
Everyone in that stadium turned
    their faces in her direction
while Marsha Cates shifted from one foot to another,
slowly lifted her French horn to her lips
her body perfectly straight beneath the burning lights.

At first the notes cracked
    like they couldn't find their place.
She stopped for a full minute
    while the crowd in the stands
shifted too. Someone snickered, pointed
but that didn't matter because soon
from out of her rented French horn
a smooth, mellow tune
lifted into the air.

Five perfect notes: A-B-G-G-D
it rang out:
    one syllable for each note
We must not forget.
We must not forget.

As Marsha Cates played,
one by one
the French horn section
joined her on the field
in an arc
golden horns raised
bodies straight, and
played the notes
over and over
and over
until everyone in that stadium
including the heroes
saw faces

in the golden notes
faces loved
faces remembered,
Collie Sims' face
and knew something
so sweet
so pure
so important
that for just
the briefest moment
no one in that stadium was a hero,
least of all Marsha Cates.

They were all just people,
loving

Biographical Notes

Diane Ackerman (1948–) Prize-winning poet and essay-ist whose writing is praised for its breadth and sensitivity.

Anna Akhmatova (1889–1966) At her death she was consid-ered the greatest woman poet in Russian literature. The pri-mary theme of her verse was tragic love.

Samuel Allen (1917–) Writing under the name Paul Vesey, Allen was a leader in African American literature and won several international awards.

Yehuda Amichai (1925–) Born in Germany, Amichai immigrated to Palestine in 1936. He is an honorary member of the American Academy and Institute of Arts and Letters.

A.R. Ammons (1926–) Critically acclaimed poet who has been praised for his lyrical, detailed insights into nature.

Kathi Appelt (1954–) Children's books are her first love, primarily because she is the mother of two sons who inspire her work.

Matsuo Basho (1644–1694) Considered Japan's greatest haiku poet, his masterpiece details a literal and literary journey into the heart of his culture and history.

Hillaire Belloc (1870–1953) This prolific British author wrote more than 150 books, including poetry, novels, essays and satires.

D.C. Berry (1942–) He has written more than three hundred poems and published several books, including *Saigon Cemetery* which was inspired by his military service in the Viet-nam War.

William Blake (1757–1827) His highly imaginative, radiant poetry appears in a unique form called 'illuminated printing'—engravings which Blake made and colored by hand.

Joseph Brodsky (1940–1995) In his acceptance speech upon winning the Nobel Prize for Literature, Brodsky shared with his predecessor, Fyodor Dostoyevsky, the belief that beauty could be the salvation of the human race.

Gelett Burgess (1866–1951) The author of many stories, plays and poems, Burgess was also admired for his suspense novels.

Biographical Notes

Robert Burns (1759–1796) Revered as the national poet of Scotland, Burns wrote brilliant narrative poems and satires as well as memorable lyric verse.

Melville Cane (1879–1980) As a lawyer, Cane represented several prominent authors, and this contact piqued his interest in poetry. He is admired for his precision and clarity.

Siv Cedering (1939–   ) Born in Sweden, she came to the United States in 1953. She has published poems, plays, essays, novels and translations.

Nirendranath Chakravarti (1924–   ) Born in India, this author of more than twenty books of poems has also been a journalist and the editor of a magazine for teenagers.

Gu Cheng (1956–   ) The son of a poet, Cheng is the youngest of the Misty Poets groups. Although born in China, Cheng lives in exile with his wife.

Children of Terezin (c.1930–1944) These young concentration-camp prisoners created poems and drawings—images of hope in the face of despair—before the Nazis sent them to their early deaths.

Lucille Clifton (1936–   ) A multi-talented writer of prose and poetry, her work honors the strength and courage of black women raising children during the period of slavery.

Elizabeth Coatsworth (1893–1986) She won the Newbery Medal in 1931 for her narrative poem "The Cat Who Went to Heaven."

Robert Peter Tristram Coffin (1892–1955) He published more than forty books, including a collection of verse, *Strange Holiness*, which won a Pulitzer Prize in 1936.

Billy Collins (1941–   ) A professor at the City University of New York, Collins's poems are widely published, and he has won many honors and awards.

Stephen Crane (1871–1900) An American novelist, short story writer and poet, Crane achieved international fame with his novel, *The Red Badge of Courage*, and his celebrity increased with the publication of his poetry which was written in an innovative style.

Robert Creeley (1926–   ) Internationally renowned poet, playwright, novelist and essayist, Creeley's poetry has been praised for its conciseness and emotional power.

Steve Crow (1949–   ) Born in Alabama, of Cherokee and Irish ancestry, Steve Crow began writing poetry in high school, attended Louisiana State University, and in 1976 he began doctoral work in English at the University of Michigan. He developed and taught a survey course in contemporary Native American literature at the University of Michigan.

e.e. cummings (1884–1962) Playwright, poet, novelist and painter, cummings' poetry reflects his visual gifts and delicate sensibility.

Jim Daniels (1956–   ) Daniels' poetry honors the lives of blue collar workers because he feels that their experiences are often excluded from the world of poetry.

Stephen Dunn (1939–   ) A former pro basketball player and advertiser copywriter, Dunn's poetry has been praised for its spare realism and conversational voice.

Russell Edson (1935–   ) has devoted himself to the American prose poem for more than 30 years. Derived from the absurd, his stories are not meaningless; they hold meanings we know but rarely acknowledge.

T.S. Eliot (1888–1965) His radical technique and unconventional subject matter reshaped early twentieth century poetry, and he won the Nobel Prize for Literature in 1948.

Gevorg Emin (1919–   ) His deep love of his native Armenia is reflected in the more than thirty books of prose and poetry he has published.

Lawrence Ferlinghetti (1919–   ) This American poet rebelled against earlier literary traditions, and was a major figure in the 1950's *beat* generation of poets. (*Beat* is short for *beatnik*, a Yiddish word for someone who rejects convention.)

Paul Fleischman (1952–   ) The son of children's author, Sidney Fleischman, Paul's musical ear can be found in his poetry, picture books and novels. He has won many awards including the Newbery Medal.

Robert Frost (1874–1963) He was the most popular American poet of his day, a four-time Pulitzer Prize-winner who was awarded a gold medal by Congress for his poetry ". . . which has enriched the culture of the United States and the philosophy of the world."

Fujiwara No Atsutada (?–961) He was a Chunagon, a State Adviser, and the son of the Udaijin, the Minister of the Right of the Emperor Daigo. The Fujiwara family, or clan, are one of the most extraordinary families that ever existed as they have provided Japan with administrators, regents, Shoguns, poets, generals, painters, philosophers and abbots.

Fujiwara No Kiyosuke (?–177) He was the son of Fujiwara no Akisuke, also a poet, and was Lord of Nagato, vice Steward of the ex-Empress, and held the Senior Fourth Court Rank. The ZOKU SHIKA SHU anthology, which he compiled at the order of the Emperor Nijo, was unfinished at the latter's death, and so it is not ranked as one of the Imperial Anthologies.

Muhammad al-Ghuzzi (1949–   ) Born in the ancient city of Qairwan, Tunisia, Al-Ghuzzi has been a teacher; he also translates Swedish poetry into Arabic.

Nikki Giovanni (1943–   ) She grew up during the civil rights struggle of the fifties and sixties, and her poetry often voices the dreams of African Americans seeking a life free of racism.

Louise Gluck (1943–   ) One of the most respected and honored contemporary poets in the United States, Gluck's work has been praised for its skillful craftsmanship.

Ronald Gross (1935–   ) He has been a visiting lecturer or professor at more than one hundred colleges, and is a distinguished leader in the educational field.

Arthur Guitarman (1871–1943) Born in Vienna, Austria, Guitarman came to America where he published more than several thousand poems for popular newspapers and magazines. He was a founder of The Poetry Society of America.

Miroslav Holub (1923–   ) This internationally recognized Czechoslovakian poet is also a medical doctor and research scientist who often uses scientific imagery in his poetry.

Langston Hughes (1902–1967) Poet, novelist, short story writer, playwright, song lyricist, radio writer, translator and lecturer, Hughes' writing celebrated the lives and aspirations of African Americans.

Evelyn Tooley Hunt began writing poetry when she was a student, but waited many years before publishing her verse. Her book *Under the Baobab Tree* describes people and scenes from different parts of the world.

Kobayashi Issa (1762–1826) Although he spent his life in urban poverty in Edo (later named Tokyo), his haiku recreate the beauty of small creatures.

Ted Joans (1928–   ) Painter, jazz musician, poet, and travel writer, Joans is also known as the only African American surrealist artist. His poetry has been praised for its honesty and vitality.

Louis Jenkins (1942–   ) After working as a laborer, Jenkins went on to become a librarian, and the founder, in 1971, of Knife River Press.

X.J. Kennedy (1929–   ) A distinguished figure in American literature, Kennedy is widely known and praised for his poetry for children as well as adults.

Klara Koettner-Benigni (1928–   ) The author of poetry and novels, this Austrian writer also writes essays about Eastern European poetry.

Karl Krolow (1915–   ) Born in Hanover, Germany, Krolow's nature poetry has been praised for its playful, lyric quality. In 1977, he won the Rainer Maria Rilke Poetry Prize, named for the great German lyric poet.

Lady Otomo of Sakanowe Nothing is known of this poet except that she was the younger sister of Otomo no Tabito, and that she was active in the early part of the eighth century.

Li-Young Lee (1957–   ) Born in Indonesia, Lee has achieved great success in America, winning many awards and fellowships.

John Lennon (1940–1980) He and Paul McCartney wrote most of the imaginative and meaningful lyrics for the Beatles. Both Lennon and the group have become icons of late twentieth century rock music.

Denise Levertov (1923–   ) Born in England, she emigrated to the United States in 1948 and has become an acclaimed literary figure. A longtime political activist, Levertov's themes range from small details of domestic life to international military atrocities.

Philip Levine (1928–   ) Born in industrial Detroit, Levine worked at several auto companies before pursuing his career as a highly-honored poet.

Vachel Lindsay (1879–1931) He felt his strongly rhythmic poetry should be performed, and his work embraced a wide variety of subjects: baseball, movies, and politics, among others.

Li Po (c.701–c.762) He is considered one of the greatest poets of the T'ang period along with Wang Wei and Tu Fu.

Gail Mack (1936–   ) She has published several books of poetry and prose for children. A journalist, she has worked on newspapers and magazines in Boston and New York, and as publicist for regional theaters in the northeast.

David McCord Born in New York, McCord published more than twenty-five books of poetry, collections of humorous verse, and essays.

Eve Merriam (1916–1992) Merriam worked as an advertising copywriter, radio writer and fashion editor before achieving enduring success as a poet and playwright.

Edna St. Vincent Millay (1892–1950) Her lyric poetry about love, death, beauty and the universe earned her early acclaim. One of her most famous poems, 'Renascence' was published when she was nineteen, and she won a Pulitzer Prize in 1923.

Lillian Moore (1909–   ) A pioneering figure in the field of children's literature, Moore headed a book club that made inexpensive paperbacks available to school children.

Marianne Moore (1887–1972) A Pulitzer Prize-winner, Moore is ranked with Emily Dickinson as one of the finest American poets. As the editor of *Dial* Magazine, she published the work of many young writers.

Moritake (1452–1540) Arakida Moritake (Japanese) The first important writer of haikai no renga. He was the head priest of the Ise Shrine.

Harold Munro (1879–1932) Munro was a minor English poet, associated with the Georgians, and an editor. His entire poetic output was published together in "Collected Poems" (1933) with an introduction by T.S. Eliot. He is best remembered for his three influential journals and for his Poetry Bookshop, a haven for intellectuals, through which he provided generous encouragement to younger poets.

Walter Dean Myers has achieved popularity and critical acclaim in his fiction and poetry for young readers. He is particularly committed to his African American audience.

Ogden Nash (1902–1971) A master of light-hearted, comic verse, Nash used his craft to cope with the complications of modern life.

Pablo Neruda (1904–1973) Poet, diplomat, politician, Neruda was internationally acclaimed for his masterful poetry. He received many awards and honors, including the Nobel Prize in Literature.

Stella Ngatho (1953–   ) Born in Kenya, Ngatho finds inspiration in the tribal rituals and songs of her native land.

Frank O'Hara (1926–1966) Poet, playwright, art critic and curator, O'Hara's *Collected Poems* won the National Book Award, only one of many honors bestowed on his work. His life was cut tragically short when he was killed by a beach taxi on the summer resort of Fire Island.

Simon Ortiz (1941–   ) Regarded as one of the finest contemporary, native American poets and short story writers, Ortiz is a member of the Acoma Pueblo Indian nation.

Kemal Ozer (1935–   ) A native of Turkey, Ozer lives in Istanbul and is one of the most prominent and prolific literary figures in his homeland.

Dorothy Parker (1893–1967) Her biting, ironic poetry and criticism gained her membership in the legendary creative group known as 'The Algonquin Roundtable.' Parker's cynical facade concealed a sensitive and generous heart.

Linda Pastan (1932–   ) A native of New York City, Pastan has won many literary awards throughout her career, beginning in college when she placed first in a national poetry contest (second place went to poet Sylvia Plath). Her poetry often reflects the pull that women feel between domesticity and art.

Ezra Pound (1885–1972) A gifted and controversial writer, Poundís "Cantos" is considered the most important long poem in early twentieth-century literature.

Jack Prelutsky (1940–   ) His whimsical, appealing poetry is enjoyed by a wide audience of young readers.

Laura E. Richards (1850–1943) Born in Boston, she grew up in a distinguished, literary family (her mother, Julia Ward Howe, wrote the famous 'Battle Hymn of the Republic.'). Richards published more than ninety books during her long career, and won a Pulitzer Prize for a biography of her mother.

Theodore Roethke (1908–1963) Although he experimented with various styles of poetry, Roethke's verse always reflected his inner life: memories of childhood and the wonder of growing things. He won the Pulitzer Prize for poetry in 1954.

Jalāl al-Dīn Rūmī (1207–1273) This Sufi (Islamic mystic) was a brilliant lyrical poet of the Persian language, whose work widely influenced Muslim mystical thought and literature. Rumi inspired a religious order, known in the West as the "Whirling Dervishes" because of the mystical dance that constitutes their principle ritual.

Carl Sandburg (1878–1967) Sandburg's Pulitzer-Prize winning poetry mirrors his love of the American heartland. A distinguished collector of American folklore, he wrote a Pulitzer Prize-winning, four-volume biography of Abraham Lincoln.

Anne Sexton (1928–1972) Her life was troubled by mental illness, but Sexton had an enduring commitment to her poetry. She won a Pulitzer Prize in 1967.

William Shakespeare (1564–1616) This English playwright and poet is considered one of the greatest writers of all time. A master of meter and meaning. Shakespeare's writing is noted for its psychological insight and complexity as well as the beauty of its language.

Karl Jay Shapiro (1913–   ) Poet and novelist, Shapiro was a champion of individuality who won a Pulitzer Prize for poetry in 1945.

Shel Silverstein (1932–   ) Although he is best known for his young people's poetry, Silverstein is also a composer, cartoonist and folksinger.

Charles Simic (1938–   ) Born in Yugoslavia, Simic has achieved considerable literary distinction in his adopted country. He has won numerous prizes, including a Pulitzer Prize in 1990.

Louis Simpson (1923–   ) This Jamican-born poet and educator has won many awards for his writing, which has been praised for its subtlety and hidden layers of meaning. He has been honored with many awards and prizes.

Hal Sirowitz (1949–   ) Born in Manhattan, Sirowitz teaches special education in the New York City public schools. He has appeared on MTV's Spoken Word Unplugged and was featured on the PBS series The United States of Poetry.

Muso Soseki (13th century) A widely revered Zen teacher, this Japanese poet had more than 13,000 students in his lifetime. He is also credited with being the creator of the original Japanese rock garden.

William Stafford (1914–1993) A dedicated pacifist, Stafford's poetry is known for its accessibility and independent craftsmanship. He has won many awards and honors.

Gertrude Stein (1874–1946) After her graduation from Radcliffe and studies with the philosopher William James, Stein moved to Paris in 1903. Stein's unique style of simple writing and her literary criticism influenced a generation of American writers, such as Hemingway and Fitzgerald.

May Swenson (1919–1989) Born in Logan, Utah, she came to New York where she worked as an editor and college lecturer. She wanted her poetry to reflect the way things actually are, not how they seem.

Sara Teasdale (1884–1933) Although her poetry reflects the sadness imposed on her from childhood, Teasdale's work has always been admired for its lyricism and craftsmanship.

John Updike (1932–   ) His elegant prose and witty poetry often deals with the conflicts of middle class life.

Derek Walcott (1930–   ) Born in St. Lucia, Walcott is the master poet of West Indian culture, a distinguished writer who won the Nobel Prize for Literature in 1992. His style is noted for its melody and sensitivity.

Margaret Walker (1915–1998) Born in Birmingham, Alabama, Walker was the daughter of college professors. Her pioneering novel, *Jubilee,* about the legacy of Africans in Americans was the inspiration for *Roots.*

John Hall Wheelock (1886–1978) He published his first book of poems while he was a student at Harvard, and continued to write until his death at 92.

E.B. White (1899–1985) Poet, novelist, newspaper reporter, and editor, White was a contributor to *The New Yorker* and *Harper's Magazine.* He wrote the children's classics, *Stuart Little, Charlotte's Web* and *The Trumpet of the Swan.*

Walt Whitman (1819–1892) Whitman's collection, *Leaves of Grass,* is considered one of the world's great literary works. His poetry reflects the joys and sorrows of life.

James Wright (1927–1980) Wright shares with William Stafford a simplicity and directness of language. His work is also distinguished by its compassion.

William Butler Yeats (1865–1939) His poetry and plays focused on Celtic, rather than English, language and culture. Considered one of the greatest lyric poets of the twentieth century, Yeats won the Nobel Prize for Literature in 1923.

Acknowledgments *(continued from p. ii)*

BOA Editions, Ltd.
Lucille Clifton: "the poet," "let there be new flowering," "prayer," "break-light," copyright © 1987 by Lucille Clifton, from *GOOD WOMAN: POEMS AND A MEMOIR 1969-1980*. Li-Young Lee: "I Ask My Mother to Sing," copyright © 1986 by Li-Young Lee, from *ROSE*. Reprinted by permission of BOA Editions, Ltd., 260 East Avenue, Rochester, NY 14604.

George Braziller, Inc. Publishers
"Fear" by Charles Simic from *Dismantling the Silence*. Copyright 1971 by Charles Simic. Reprinted by permission of George Braziller, Inc. Publishers.

Curtis Brown Ltd.
"Invisible Cat" from *Ghastlies, Goops & Pincushions: Nonsense Verse* by X.J. Kennedy. Published by Margaret K. McElderry Books, an imprint of Simon & Schuster Books for Young Readers. Reprinted by permission of Curtis Brown, Ltd. Copyright © 1989 by X.J. Kennedy.

Siv Cedering
"When It Is Snowing" by Siv Cedering from *The Juggler*, published by Sagarin Press. Copyright © 1977 by Siv Cedering. Reprinted by permission of the author.

Nirendranath Chakravarti
"The Garden of a Child" by Nirendranath Chakravarti. Copyright © 1992 by Nirendranath Chakravarti. Reprinted by permission of the author.

Gu Cheng
"Far and Close" by Gu Cheng, translated by Edward Morin, from *Heiyanjing*, copyright © 1986 by Gu Cheng.

The Christian Science Monitor
"Unfolding Bud" from July 3, 1957 issue of *The Christian Science Monitor*. Copyright © 1957 The Christian Science Publishing Society. All rights reserved. Reprinted with permission from The Christian Science Monitor.

Mrs. Robert P.T. Coffin, Jr., Richard Coffin and Vernon C. Westcott
"Forgive My Guilt" by Robert P. Tristram Coffin, copyright 1949 by The Atlantic Monthly Co. Reprinted by permission of Mrs. Robert P.T. Coffin, Jr., Richard Coffin and Vernon C. Westcott.

Columbia University Press
"The Pen" by Muhammed al-Ghuzzi from *Modern Arabic Poetry, An Anthology* ed. Salma Khadra Jayyusi, © 1987 Columbia University Press. Reprinted with the permission of the publisher.

Copper Canyon Press
"What Is It That Upsets the Volcanoes" ("VIII") from *The Book of Questions* © 1991 by Pablo Neruda, translated by William O'Daly. Reprinted by permission of Copper Canyon Press, Post Office Box 271, Port Townsend, WA 98368.

Steve Crow
"Revival" by Steve Crow from *Harper's Anthology of 20th Century Native American Poetry* by Duane Niatum. Copyright © 1988 by Duane Niatum. Reprinted by permission of the author.

Crown Publishers, Inc.
"Deformed Finger" from *Mother Said* by Hal Sirowitz. Copyright © 1996 by Hal Sirowitz. Reprinted by permission of Crown Publishers.

Jim Daniels
"Baseball Cards #1" from *The Long Ball* by Jim Daniels. Copyright © by Jim Daniels. Reprinted by permission of the author.

Diana Der-Hovanessian
"The Question Mark" by Gevorg Emin from *For You On New Year's Day*, translated by Diana Der-Hovanessian, published by Ohio University Press, copyright © Diana Der-Hovanessian. Reprinted by permission of the translator.

Doubleday, a division of Random House, Inc.
"Fallen flowers rise" by Moritake and " A lightning gleam" by Matsuo Basho from *An Introduction to Haiku* by Harold G. Henderson. Copyright © 1958 by Harold G. Henderson. "The Sloth," copyright 1950 by Theodore Roethke, from *The Collected Poems of Theodore Roethke* by Theodore Roethke. Used by permission of Doubleday, a division of Random House, Inc.

The Ecco Press
"Gratitude" from *The House on Marshland* by Louise Glück. Copyright © 1971, 1972, 1973, 1974, 1975 by Louise Glück. Reprinted by permission of The Ecco Press.

Russell Edson
"The Wounded Breakfast" by Russell Edson. Reprinted by permission of the author.

Farrar, Straus & Giroux, Inc.
"Midsummer, Tobago" from *Complete Poems 1948–1984* by Derek Walcott. Copyright © 1986 by Derek Walcott. Reprinted by permission of Farrar, Straus & Giroux, Inc. "Sir, You Are Tough" by Joseph Brodsky.

Franklin Watts
"Chocolates" by Louis Simpson from *Caviare at the Funeral*. Copyright © 1980 by Louis Simpson. Reprinted by permission of the publisher, Franklin Watts.

Gnomon Press
"only one guy and" by Issa, translated by Cid Corman from *One Man's Moon: Fifty Haiku*, Gnomon Press, 1984. Reprinted by permission of the publisher.

Graywolf Press
"First Grade" copyright 1987, 1998 by the Estate of William Stafford. Reprinted from *The Way It Is: New & Selected Poems* by William Stafford with the permission of Graywolf Press, Saint Paul, Minnesota.

Donald Hall for the Estate of Jane Kenyon
"Everything Promised Him to Me" from *Twenty Poems of Anna Akhmatova*, translated by Jane Kenyon and Vera Dunham; The Eighties/Ally Press; St. Paul, MN. Copyright © Estate of Jane Kenyon. Reprinted by permission of Donald Hall for the Estate of Jane Kenyon.

Harcourt Brace & Company
"Window" and "Lost" from *Chicago Poems* by Carl Sandburg, copyright 1916 by Holt, Rinehart and Winston and renewed 1944 by Carl Sandburg. "Buffalo Dusk" from *Smoke and Steel* by Carl Sandburg, copyright 1920 by Harcourt Brace & Company and renewed 1948 by Carl Sandburg. "Splinter" from *Good Morning, America*, copyright 1928 and renewed 1956 by Carl Sandburg. "Washington Monument by Night" from *Slabs of the Sunburnt West* by Carl Sandburg, copyright 1922 by Harcourt Brace & Company and renewed 1950 by Carl Sandburg. Reprinted by permission of Harcourt Brace & Company.

Harcourt Brace & Company and Faber & Faber Ltd.
"The Rum Tum Tugger" from *Old Possum's Book of Practical Cats*, copyright 1939 by T.S. Eliot and renewed 1967 by Esme Valerie Eliot, reprinted by permission of Harcourt Brace & Company and Faber & Faber Ltd., publishers.

Acknowledgments

Faber & Faber Ltd.
"Preludes" by T.S. Eliot from *Collected Poems 1909-1962* by T.S. Eliot. Reprinted by permission of Faber & Faber Ltd., publisher.

HarperCollins Publishers, Inc.
"Natural History" from *Poems and Sketches of E.B. White* by E.B. White. Copyright 1929 by E.B. White. Reprinted by permission of HarΔperCollins Publishers, Inc.

HarperCollins Publishers
"Listen to the Mustn'ts" from *Where the Sidewalk Ends* by Shel Silverstein. Copyright © 1974 by Evil Eye Music, Inc. "Mayflies" from *Joyful Noise* by Paul Fleischman. Text copyright © 1988 by Paul Fleischman. "The Passenger Pigeon" from *I Am Phoenix* by Paul Fleischman. Text copyright © 1985 by Paul Fleischman. "Summer" from *Brown Angels: An Album of Pictures and Verse* by Walter Dean Myers. Copyright © 1993 by Walter Dean Myers. Used by permission of HarperCollins Publishers.

Henry Holt & Company
"The Secret Sits" from *The Poetry of Robert Frost*, edited by Edward Connery Lathem, Copyright 1942 by Robert Frost. Copyright 1970 by Lesley Frost Ballantine. © 1969 by Henry Holt & Company. "The Span of Life" and "Acquainted With the Night" from *The Poetry of Robert Frost*, edited by Edward Connery Lathem. Copyright 1936, 1956 by Robert Frost. Copyright 1964 by Lesley Frost Ballantine. Copyright 1928, © 1969 by Henry Holt & Company. Reprinted by permission of Henry Holt & Company.

Houghton Mifflin Company
"The Fury of Overshoes" from *The Death Notebooks*. Copyright © 1974 by Anne Sexton. Reprinted by permission of Houghton Mifflin Company. All Rights Reserved.

Yuka Igarashi
"First Day Back" by Yuka Igarashi. Reprinted by permission of the author.

Janklow & Nesbit Assoicates for Diane Ackerman
"Patrick Ewing Takes a Foul Shot" by Diane Ackerman, originally published by William Morrow & Co., Inc.

Louis Jenkins
"Too Much Snow" by Louis Jenkins from *Just Above Water*. Copyright 1997 by Louis Jenkins. Reprinted by permission of the author.

Johnson Publishing
"Mama is a Sunrise" by Evelyn Tooley Hunt from *The Lyric*.

Ted Joans
"Voice in the Crowd" by Ted Joans. Copyright © 19??.

Alfred A. Knopf, Inc.
"Dressed Up" from *Collected Poems* by Langston Hughes. Copyright © 1994 by the Estate of Langston Hughes. "M Degas Teaches Art & Science at Durfee Intermediate School" from *What Work Is* by Philip Levine. Copyright © 1991 by Philip Levine. "Autobiographia Literaria" from *Collected Poems* by Frank O'Hara. Copyright © 1967 by Maureen Granville-Smith, Administratix of the Estate of Frank O'Hara. "Player Piano" from *The Carpentered Hen and Other Tame Creatures* by John Updike. Copyright 1954 by John Updike. "Dream Boogie" from *Collected Poems* by Langston Hughes. Copyright © 1994 by the Estate of Langston Hughes. Reprinted by permisssion of Alfred A. Knopf, Inc.

Peters Fraser and Dunlop on behalf of the Estate of Hillaire Belloc
"The Vulture" by Hillaire Belloc from *Complete Verse* (Pimlico, a division of Random Century). Copyright 1931 by Hillaire Belloc. Copyright © renewed

1959 by Eleanor Jebb Belloc, Elizabeth Belloc, and Hilary Belloc. Reprinted by permission of Peters Fraser and Dunlop on behalf of the Estate of Hillaire Belloc.

The Literary Estate of May Swenson
"Analysis of Baseball" by May Swenson. First appeared in *American Sports Poems* (Orchard Press, 1989). Used with permission of The Literary Estate of May Swenson.

Klara Koettner-Benigni and Herbert Kuhner
"Monkeys" by Klara Koettner-Benigni, translated by Herbert Kuhner. Copyright © Klara Koettner-Benigni and Herbert Kuhner. Reprinted by permission of the author and the translator.

Karl Krolow
"The Open Shutter" by Karl Krolow. Copyright © by Karl Krolow.

Little, Brown and Company
"Ode to the Cat" from *Odes to Common Things* by Pablo Neruda. Copyright © 1994 by Pablo Neruda and Pablo Neruda Foundation. (Odes in Spanish); Compilation and Illustrations © by Ferris Cook (English Translation) © by Ken Krabbenhoft. "Crows" from *Far and Few* by David McCord. Copyright © 1952 by David McCord. "Eletelephony" from *Tirra Lirra* by Laura Richards. Copyright © 1930, 1932 by Laura E. Richards, copyright © renewed 1960 by Hamilton Richards. "The Octopus" from *Verses From 1929 On* by Ogden Nash. Copyright © 1942 by Ogden Nash, first appeared in The New Yorker. "A Caution to Everybody" from *Verses from 1929 On* by Ogden Nash. Copyright 1950 by Odgen Nash; copyright © renewed 1977 by Frances Nash, Isabel Nash Eberstadt, and Linnell Nash Smith. First appeared in Hearsts' International Cosmopolitan. Reprinted by permission of Little, Brown and Company.

Liveright Publishing
"who are you, little i", copyright © 1963, 1991 by the Trustees for the E. E. Cummings Trust, from *Complete Poems: 1904-1962* by E. E. Cummings. Edited by George J. Firmage. Reprinted by permission of Liveright Publishing Corporation.

Gail Kredenser Mack
"The Cardinal in the Birdbath" by Gail Kredenser Mack. Reprinted by permission of the author.

Freda McGregor
"Overheard on a Saltmarsh" by Harold Monro. Reprinted by permission of Freda McGregor.

M.S. Merwin and Soiku Shigematsu
"House of Spring" by Muso Soseki from *Sun at Midnight,* translated by W.S. Merwin and Soiku Shigematsu, published by North Point Press, San Francisco, copyright © 1989 by W.S. Merwin. Reprinted by permission of the translator, M.S. Merwin.

Greenwillow Books, a division of William Morrow & Co., Inc.
"I Think My Computer Is Crazy," "A Pizza the Size of the Sun" and "I'm Drifting Through Negative Space" from *a PIZZA the Size of the SUN* poems by Jack Prelutsky. Text copyright © 1994, 1996 by Jack Prelutsky. "Knoxville, Tennessee" by Nikki Giovanni from *Black Feeling, Black Talk, Black Judgement.* Copyright 1968, 1970 by Nikki Giovanni. Reprinted by permission of Greenwillow Books, a division of William Morrow & Co., Inc.

New Directions Publishing Corp.
"Fortune" by Lawrence Ferlinghetti from *A Coney Island of the Mind.* Copyright © 1958 by Lawrence Ferlinghetti. "Sandinista Avioncitos" by

Acknowledgments

Lawrence Ferlinghetti from *These Are My Rivers.* Copyright © 1993 by Lawrence Ferlinghetti. "The Secret" by Denise Levertov from *Poems 1960-1967.* Copyright © 1964 by Denise Levertov. "You Say 'I Will Come'" by Lady Otomo No Sakanoe, "I May Live On Until" by Fujiwara No Kiyosuke and "I Think of the Days" by Fujiwara No Atsutada from *One Hundred Poems from the Japanese,* translated by Kenneth Rexroth. Copyright © All Rights Reserved by New Directions Publishing. "Meditatio" by Ezra Pound from *Personae.* Copyright © 1926 by Ezra Pound. "Six Variations (Part III)" by Denise Levertov from *Poems 1960-1967.* Copyright © 1966 by Denise Levertov. Reprinted by permission of New Directions Publishing Corp.

Stella Ngatho

"Footpath" by Stella Ngatho from *This Same Sky.* Copyright © by Stella Ngatho.

W.W. Norton & Company, Inc.

"Happiness," copyright © 1989 by Stephen Dunn, from *New and Selected Poems 1974-1994* by Stephen Dunn. "Reflective" copyright © 1965 by A.R. Ammons, from *The Selected Poems, Expanded Edition* by A.R. Ammons. "Winter Scene" copyright © 1968 by A.R. Ammons, from *The Selected Poems, Expanded Edition* by A.R. Ammons. "To A Daughter Leaving Home," from *The Imperfect Paradise* by Linda Pastan. Copyright © 1988 by Linda Pastan. Reprinted by permission of W.W. Norton & Company, Inc.

Simon J. Ortiz

"My Father's Song" by Simon Ortiz from *Going for the Rain: Poems by Simon J. Ortiz.* Copyright © 1976 by Simon J. Ortiz. Reprinted by permission of the author.

Kemal Ozer and Cynthia Riggs for the Estate of Dionis Riggs

"At the Beach" by Kemal Ozer, translated by O. Yalim, W. Fielder, and Dionis Riggs. Copyright © by Kemal Ozer and Dionis Riggs. Reprinted by permission of Kemal Ozer and Cynthia Riggs for the Estate of Dionis Riggs.

Peter Owen Ltd., London

"A Very Valentine" by Gertrude Stein from *Writings and Lectures 1911-1945.* Reprinted by permission of Peter Owen Ltd., London.

Marian Reiner

"How to Eat a Poem" from *It Doesn't Always Have to Rhyme* by Eve Merriam. Copyright © 1964 Eve Merriam. Copyright renewed 1992 Eve Merriam. "Parking Lot Full" from *Rainbow Writing* by Eve Merriam. Copyright © 1976 by Eve Merriam. "New Love" from *Fresh Paint* by Eve Merriam. Copyright © 1986 by Eve Merriam. Reprinted by permission of Marian Reiner.

Marian Reiner for the author

"Said A Long Crocodile" from *See My Lovely Poison Ivy* by Lilian Moore. Copyright © 1975 by Lilian Moore. Used by permission of Marian Reiner for the author.

Schocken Books, distributed by Pantheon Books, a division of Random House, Inc.

"On a Sunny Evening," by The Children in Barracks L 318 and L 417, Terezin Concentration Camp from *I Never Saw Another Butterfly, Expanded 2nd Edition* by Hana Volavkova (editor). Copyright © 1978, 1993 by Artia, Prague. Compilation copyright © 1993 by Schocken Books, Inc. Foreword copyright © 1993 by Chaim Potok. Reprinted by permission of Schocken Books, distributed by Pantheon Books, a division of Random House, Inc.

Louise H. Sclove

"Ancient History" from *Lyric Laughter* by Arthur Guiterman, copyright 1939 by E.P. Dutton & Co., Inc.

Acknowledgments

Scribner, a division of Simon & Schuster
"Earth" reprinted with the permission of Scribner, a division of Simon & Schuster from *The Gardener and Other Poems* by John Hall Wheelock. Copyright © 1961 by John Hall Wheelock, renewed 1989 by Sally Wheelock Brayton.

Simon & Schuster Books for Young Readers, an imprint of Simon & Schuster Children's Publishing Division
"The Rabbits' Song Outside the Tavern" and "Swift Things are Beautiful" reprinted with the permission of Simon & Schuster Books for Young Readers, an imprint of Simon & Schuster Children's Publishing Division from *Away Goes Sally* by Elizabeth Coatsworth. Copyright 1934 Macmillan Publishing Company; copyright renewed © 1962 Elizabeth Coatsworth Beston.

Simon & Schuster
"Yield" from *Pop Poems* by Ronald Gross. Copyright © 1967 by Ronald Gross. "The Moon's the North Wind's Cooky" from *The Collected Poems of Vachel Lindsay.* Copyright 1925 by Macmillan Publishing Company, renewed 1953 by Elizabeth C. Lindsay. "Night" and "The Falling Star" from *The Collected Poems of Sara Teasdale.* Copyright 1930 by Sara Teasdale Filsinger; copyright renewed ©1958 by Guaranty Trust Co. of New York, Executor. "Silence" from *The Collected Poems of Marianne Moore.* Copyright 1935 by Marianne Moore; copyright renewed © 1963 by Marianne Moore and T.S. Eliot. Reprinted by permission of Simon & Schuster.

Sony/ATV Music Publishing
"Eleanor Rigby," words and music by John Lennon and Paul McCartney. Copyright © 1966 Sony/ATV Songs LLC (Renewed). All rights administered by Sony/ATV Music Publishing, 8 Music Square West, Nashville, TN 37203. All Rights Reserved. Used by permission.

Stanford University Press
"The Firefly" by Li Tai Po is reprinted from *A Garden of Peonies,* translated by Henry H. Hart with the permission of the publishers, Stanford University Press. Copyright © 1938 by the Board of Trustees of the Leland Stanford Junior University. Copyright renewed 1966 by Henry S. Hart.

Michael Stillman
"In Memoriam John Coltrane" by Michael Stillman from *Occident,* Fall 1971, Berkeley. Copyright © 1971 by Michael Stillman. Reprinted by permission of the author.

Threshold Books
"Who Makes These Changes?" from *The Essential Rumi* by Jalal al-Din Rumi, translated by Coleman Barks, with John Moyne, A. J. Arberry, and Reynold Nicholson. Copyright © 1995 by Coleman Barks. Originally published by Threshold Books, 139 Main Street, Brattleboro, VT 05301. Reprinted by permission of Threshold Books.

University of California Press
"Oh No" from *Collected Poems of Robert Creeley, 1945-1975,* edited by Sharon Zukin. Copyright © by Robert Creeley. Reprinted by permission of the publisher, University of California Press.

Regents of the University of California and the University of California Press
"Jerusalem" from *The Selected Poetry of Yehuda Amichai,* edited and translated by Chana Bloch and Stephen Mitchell. Copyright © 1996 The Regents of the University of California. Reprinted by permission of the Regents of the University of California and the University of California Press.

Acknowledgments

University of Georgia Press

"Lineage" from *This is My Century: New and Collected Poems* by Margaret Alexander Walker. Copyright © 1989 by Margaret Alexander Walker. Published by University of Georgia Press (Athens, GA). Reprinted by permission of the publisher.

University of Pittsburgh Press

"On Turning Ten" is from *The Art of Drowning*, by Billy Collins, © 1995. Reprinted by permission of the University of Pittsburgh Press.

University Press of New England

James Wright "A Blessing" from *Above the River: The Complete Poems* © 1990 by Anne Wright, Wesleyan University Press, by permission of University Press of New England.

Viking Penguin, a division of Penguin Putnam

"Unfortunate Coincidence," copyright 1926, © renewed 1954 by Dorothy Parker, from *The Portable Dorothy Parker* by Dorothy Parker. Used by permission of Viking Penguin, a division of Penguin Putnam Inc. "A Boy's Head" by Miroslav Holub translated by Ian Milner from *Selected Poems,* published by Viking Penguin, copyright © 1967 Miroslav Holub, and "Napoleon," copyright © 1992 by Miroslav Holub.

Wiesner & Wiesner, Inc., NY

"Interlude III" by Karl Shapiro from *Poems 1940-1953*. Copyright © 1978, 1987 Karl Shapiro. Reprinted by arrangement with Wiesner & Wiesner, Inc., NY.

Note: Every effort has been made to locate the copyright owner of material reprinted in this book. Omissions brought to our attention will be corrected in subsequent editions.